Serendipitous

Turning Chance into Possibilities

Prof. Rabindra Chandra Bhattacharya

ALLIED PUBLISHERS PVT. LTD.

New Delhi • Mumbai • Kolkata • Chennai • Bangalore • Hyderabad

ALLIED PUBLISHERS PRIVATE LIMITED

D-5, Sector-2, **Noida**–201 301
Ph. Nos.: 0120-4320295/2542557/4352866
E-mail: delhi.books@alliedpublishers.com

17 Chittaranjan Avenue, **Kolkata**–700072
Ph.: 033-22129618 • E-mail: cal.books@alliedpublishers.com

15 J.N. Heredia Marg, Ballard Estate, **Mumbai**–400001
Ph.: 022-42126969 • E-mail: mumbai.books@alliedpublishers.com

No. 25/10, Commander-in-Chief Road, Ethiraj Lane (Next to Post Office)
Egmore, **Chennai**–600008
Ph.: 044-28223938 • E-mail: chennai.books@alliedpublishers.com

P.B. No. 9932, No. 15, 3rd Floor (Next to Vijaya Bank), 5th Cross, Gandhinagar,
Karnataka, **Bangalore**–560009. Ph.: 080-41530285 / 22386239
• E-mail: bngl.journals@alliedpublishers.com / apsabng@airtelmail.in

Sri Jayalakshmi Nilayam, No. 3-4-510, 3rd Floor (Above More Super Market)
Barkatpura, **Hyderabad**–500027
Ph.: 040-27551811, 040-27551812 • E-mail: hyd.books@alliedpublishers.com

Website: www.alliedpublishers.com

ISBN: 978-93-5607-291-6

Inspiration: My daughters, Sutapa & Sumita
Illustration: A. Das

Published by Sunil Sachdev and printed by Ravi Sachdev
at Allied Publishers Pvt. Ltd., D-5, Sector-2, Noida–201 301

Dedication

"This book is dedicated to my grandmother who introduced me to the great Indian Scriptures although she was unlettered, and to my grandchildren, Ashika, Akash, and Megha in the hope that one day they will reflect on grandpa's musings and appreciate their heritage".

Preface

Almost everything in my life has been unexpected. As a village boy, having seen, experienced and even enjoyed nothing beyond the vast rivers and ponds, the lush green of undivided Bengal, and the innocent joys and travails of a typical Bengali village life, the only thing I somehow knew was that I did not belong here. I was meant to be some where else, doing something else. This could not be my life.

What transpired across my life has been a series of events and occurrences that came on my way as they did, unexpectedly and I took each one, accepted and completed with passion to the best of my ability. With gratitude too, because in retrospect, as if with serendipity, eventually, all the pieces came together to live an unexpected, but good life.

Every time an opportunity or a challenge arose, I would grasp the situation and try to make the best of it. When someone told me of the need to do a course, I took it on, when someone questioned my ability, I took it on, when someone opened a window, I opened the door.

85 years ago, never could I have expected, that I would visit as many countries as I did, work till the ripe old age of 85, experience so many adventures, meet so many people, as I have done, l learned so much, and still have the passion to live with purpose and with hope.

It is said that 200,000 people die daily but every day that we wake up to life, unexpected as it may be, is a blessing and a gift.

I am deeply thankful for this gift of the life that I have been given and for whatever little I have been able to impart and share in my years in service and teaching.

I am grateful for the unexpected friends that I have met on this journey of life, for the knowledge that I have gained, for the love that I have received—for the little boy who had felt ever so unloved and unnoticed in his childhood days.

At the end of it all, mine has been an ordinary life, one may say, but in so many ways, extraordinary. But isn't that the way of all our lives? Each is unique, each ordinary, yet uniquely extraordinary.

Acknowledgement

My life is a journey of a remote village boy from Bangladesh through ups and downs. I had never thought that this simple story was worth publishing.

From their childhood, my daughters have heard me speaking about my travails in life. They were the key people who insisted that I jot these memories into a book.

Although there were ups and downs, I never felt bad about it. In fact, I used to look upon my past as a spectator, as if it was happening to someone else. After every down, there was always an up. As I look back, I feel as if providence was always there ready with a helping hand whenever I faced any problem.

This book would have never seen the light but for the constant encouragement of my daughters, Sutapa and Sumita both of whom are like my friends. They knew every detail. Yet they insisted that I write a book on my life's journey. In fact, it is my elder daughter, Sutapa who without my knowledge arranged for a writer, to type this book as I dictated. I visit her every year in Kuala Lumpur. So, in 2018, she arranged for Mr. Yong Hee, a young writer. We would meet at a coffee shop and I would relate to him the story of my life and later he used to type out these notes. Next year, in 2019, the same thing happened and this was how the manuscript began to take shape.

I also spoke about my life's journey to my students and some close friends, mainly as examples and case studies. Some of them also requested me to write something for posterity. One of my ex-colleagues, Prof. Prabir Guha happens to be a prolific writer. He also encouraged me to write a book.

I had the privilege of introducing two new courses at IIMC. The first was on Industrial Marketing in 1986 and the other was on Services Marketing in 1991. At that time, there were hardly any books on these topics. Many publishers approached me to write books on these topics. But I did not have the courage to write books lest I showed my ignorance.

I only jotted down some stray thoughts from my memory. My elder daughter, Sutapa has tried to give shape to these thoughts. So, most of the credit goes to her. My younger daughter, Sumita, has chosen the title. I am grateful to her. My wife, Sabita stood by me although she says everybody who knows me already know these stories.

At long last, the book is seeing the light of the day because one of my former students, Prof. (Dr.) Rajdeep Bakshi took the responsibility of mentoring me in publishing this book.

So, I thank my daughters Sutapa and Sumita, my wife, Prof. Prabir Guha and Prof. (Dr.) Rajdeep Bakshi. I am also indebted to all others who have listened to these stories as my students, colleagues, friends and all those who crossed my life and shaped it through encouragement or sometimes expressing disbelief in my capability. I am also indebted to the artist Mr. Arpan Das who took pains in creating the many sketches based on my thoughts and Mr. Jawed Hossain who eventually designed the cover design.

Finally, I thank Mr. Bikram Dasgupta for giving me an opportunity at GBS (Globsyn Business School) for doing whatever I could contribute for the institution and the education sector. I also thank Mr. Rahul Dasgupta for going through the manuscript and giving some valuable suggestions. I am sure he will take the school to even greater heights in the future.

I have done whatever came my way and I think I am done. Now, the only thing I seek to know is the fourth state of mind, Turya by which one can know the meaning of Eternity and the Ultimate Reality.

Contents

Preface .... *vii*

Acknowledgement .... *ix*

Part I: Initial Days

1. The Beginning 3
2. Village Life 11
3. School, Family and Friends 20
4. Father's Business Life 30
5. The Partition 33

Part II: Life after Bangladesh

6. Agartala Days 39
7. Tryst with M.Sc. 48

Part III: Early Work Life

8. Life after Kolkata 59
9. Life Outside Tata Motors 70
10. My Marriage 75

Part IV: Life after Marriage

11. My Family 81
12. Time after Howrah City Engineering 84

Part V: Life in UK

13. Days in England 101
14. Days in Cranfield 117

Part VI: Back Home in India

15. Journey at IOL (BOC-India) 129
16. Back to the Gases Division 153
17. Life after IOL 158

Part VII: My Entry into Academics

18. Entry into Academics 165

Part VIII: Eternal Search

19. The Eternal Search for Meaning in Life 193

PART-I

Initial Days

With My Life Companion on My 75th Birthday

1

The Beginning

My forefathers came from a place called Kannauj under the United Province (UP) district, in Northern part of India. We are a Brahmin family and perhaps, at one time, my forefathers looked for a better future and came to settle down at the Eastern part of undivided Bengal, now known as Bangladesh. The Bengal province is in the eastern part of India. The province was intentionally divided by the British in 1905 to "tame" and subjugate the intellectual and educated Bengalis who were at the forefront of leading the freedom movement against the harsh British rule in India.

Our family migrated from UP to Bangladesh sixteen generations ago. I know this because we had a family tree. It was given to me by my uncle, Late Barada Kanta Bhattacharjee (Bhattacharjee and Bhattacharya are the same) for preservation. Over time, as we moved home from place to place, I lost the family tree document.

Our main profession as a family was priesthood. In fact, the title, Bhattacharya (or Bhattacharjee) means priest. The priest class had never been paid much for their services. Though we had a reasonable amount of cultivable land in our village, Austagram under Mymensingh district of Bangladesh, it was only enough for our basic grain requirement. We had quite a number of cows. So, we also had enough milk for the family. But we always felt a scarcity of other food stuff and daily necessities apart from the basic grains and milk.

The agricultural income alone was not enough to feed and sustain thirty odd family members, including my grandmother, uncles, aunts, cousins, servants and maids. So, some male family members always had to leave home to work and earn in nearby towns by doing odd-jobs like writing expense books, keeping accounts etc. and helping businessmen in those towns.

At that time, Myanmar (then known as Burma) was a fashionable place to go for Indians to make a fortune. My grandfather, late Rajani Kanta Bhattacharjee went to Myanmar, a foreign country far away from Bangladesh in search of making his fortune. He was a person from a middle-class family, that too from a remote village in Bangladesh. It was definitely a courageous act at that time to go to a foreign country to seek a fortune.

My grandfather took this step, mainly to pay for the education of his younger brother, Mahendra Bhattacharjee, on whom the family placed great hope. My grandfather was a staunch Brahmin. It used to take seven days to reach Myanmar from Calcutta (now known as Kolkata) by sea in those days. During the whole journey, he did not eat a morsel of food, nor even drink a drop of water as it was considered wrong to accept food or water from people of other castes and religions. He survived two such return journeys. But on the third trip, during his return journey from Myanmar, he fell ill and died on reaching the shores of Kolkata.

Hence, my grandfather's younger brother, Mahendra, had to discontinue his education and instead took up a job at a spinning mill making clothing material at Ahmedabad, near Bombay in the western part of India in a state called Gujarat. This was a very faraway place from Bangladesh. Initially, he joined as an apprentice, learning the skill on the job while working.

Bengalis were well thought of and accorded social respect in those days for their professionalism. Mahendra Babu (Babu meaning Sir) told me of a personal incident. While working as an apprentice at Ahmedabad one of his senior colleagues from Gujarat got married. During the marriage procession, Mahendra Babu was requested to lead the procession as a mark of respect as he was a person from Bengal although he was a mere stipendiary.

From his meager stipend, he had to send money to his home in East Bengal (now known as Bangladesh) for the family's expenses. So, he had to control his own cost of living. He used to take low cost germinated-grams for breakfast and crushed grams known as *Sattu* as food for lunch. In this way, he used to keep his body fit while spending as little as possible.

The Mohini Cotton Mills (Kushtia, Bangladesh)

He used to exercise daily to stay fit. After the technical training as an apprentice, he took up a job in a textile mill near Kolkata.

Over time, he had become very proficient in the textile industry and ultimately became a very senior executive at the Dhakeswari Cotton Mills, Dhaka, capital of Bangladesh. This was a renowned factory in the textile industry then.

Soon, his name spread as a good textile technologist and as an able administrator. He was invited by Mr. Mohini Mohon Chakraborty, an industrialist from Bangladesh, to install a new textile plant at a place called Kushtia in Bangladesh bordering Kolkata. Mahendra, by then known as Mahendra Babu performed his job so well and Mohini Babu was so happy with him that he appointed him as the General Manager in charge of the whole plant.

In India, surnames are derived from the name of their ancestors. The original person from whom our family roots started was known as Kashyap, a well-known sage of that time. It was many thousands of years ago. Anyone, whose progeny was Kashyap, would be known as a Chatterjee. So, we were Chatterjees. But, because my forefathers took up priesthood as a living profession, we were given the title, Bhattacharjee (meaning priest). So, the surname Bhattacharjee (or Bhattacharya) is a given name and not a true family name. Obviously, Mahendra Babu was known as Mahendra Bhattacharjee. But, the owner of the new textile mill, Mohini Mohon Chakraborty, was so impressed with his achievement that he requested Mahendra Babu to change his surname to Chakraborty. Hence, Mahendra Babu and his children adopted the title Chakraborty, although the rest of our family remained as Bhattacharjee (or Bhattacharya).

When Mahendra Babu worked at textile mills near Calcutta in the early days, my father, Ranada used to stay with him and study at a local school. My father was a body builder and needed more protein to maintain his body. But the family allocation of milk was not enough for his needs. Mahendra Babu's wife, his aunt was surprised that the milk was disappearing from the kitchen although the usual amount was being purchased every day. One day, she kept watch. She found that in the afternoon, when everybody was resting, my father was drinking milk by drawing the milk with a rubber pipe from outside the kitchen through the window.

When she complained about this to Mahendra Babu after his return from office in the evening, he increased the quantity of milk to be purchased so that my father had enough milk for his requirement. Mahendra Babu was kind and fair.

My father being caught by Mahendra Babu's wife while drinking milk using a rubber pipe from outside the kitchen

Some company clerks in Mohini Mills at Kushtia used to live together in a rented house (known as mess) and had a common kitchen. One day, these clerks met the General Manager, Mahendra Babu and complained that one of the clerks was consuming half the *daal* (pulse) meant for all of them. Mahendra Babu called the clerk and asked why he was taking so much *daal* so that others were not getting enough. He answered that he was a body builder and needed more protein. So, he was taking more *daal* as protein. He said that after all, he was asking for only cheap *daal* and not asking for more fish or meat which were costly items. He was only consuming affordable *daal* for his protein requirement. Mahendra Babu asked for the clerk to be given more *daal* for his needs and he granted some amount from his own income to make the payment for the extra pulse provision. Such was his kind nature.

I remember another example in our village. There was a poor widow in our village. She had only one daughter in the family. She arranged for her daughter to marry a person called Satish Biswas on condition that he would leave his parents and stay with the in-law's family as if he was their own son. We call this system *Ghar-Jamai* or home son-in-law. Unfortunately, the daughter died prematurely. The old lady became dependent on Satish Babu who was himself poor and unable to help his mother-in-law. On hearing this, Mahendra Babu arranged to send Rupees Ten per month for the upkeep of old Mrs. Biswas for as long as she lived. Later on, when I grew up, I asked Mahendra Babu why he was giving the widow money every month although she was not related. And, if he gave the money at all, why a meager sum of Rs. 10/- only. It was 1940, Rs. 10/- must have been worth much then. But, to me, it appeared to be a very small sum. He answered that he had a duty in society to help a poor widow from his own village. If God had wanted, he could have given enough to her. But he had chosen to make her a poor person in this life time. Perhaps, it was because she had done some wrong in her past life. He gave an example to justify his action. He said that if the king of a land imprisoned someone for a crime, the prisoner would be provided enough food only to sustain and persist. At that time, if someone offered the prisoner a princely feast, would the king like it? No, I had replied. So, he said, he was only giving enough money for the widow to remain alive and endure the punishment awarded by God but not more than that.

My father was very sharp academically and always ranked first in his class. Mahendra Babu wanted my father to become an auto mechanic after finishing school. Cars were a fashionable item for the rich on those days, which were being imported from the UK. So, it was not a bad idea. But car mechanics were thought of as blue colored workmen, not very much appreciated in society. My father preferred to follow the footprints of his uncle. He revolted and joined a textile mill near Kolkata after finishing school and over time, he became a very good textile technologist. People say that my father was a better textile technologist than his uncle, Mahendra Babu.

In my early childhood, we used to stay at my father's official quarter at a place called Barrackpore, near Kolkata. He held the position of spinning master. I remember an incident that happened at Barrackpore. Once my uncle, Barada came for a holiday there. One afternoon, I was playing with a small rubber ball by myself in the room. Unmindful that my uncle was taking a nap in the adjoining room, I was making some noise. He got up and took a small stick and started beating around me but not on me. I was not hurt but was very afraid. I had a weak constitution and was very lean and thin. Out of fear, I started crying. So, he let me off the hook. He never beat me again. But I was always afraid and careful around him in future and used to treat him with reverence and awe.

Unlike my father who used to speak his mind, Barada was obedient to his uncle, Mahendra Babu. He was his favorite nephew. Although he was not that good academically, he was allowed to join college to study intermediate law. He could not pass the final law examination. So, Mahendra Babu kept him at his house and helped him to become a sub-agent of clothes of Mohini Mills which used to give him a nice flow of steady earnings. Mahendra Babu was a religious person and a devotee of a well-known sage known as Kathia Baba. Barada was a follower of Mahendra Babu. He also became a disciple of Kathia Baba order. Mahendra Babu used to like Barada like his own son. His own son, Tarak Chakraborty was more materialistic and went to Kolkata to start a business. He always lived separately from his father.

After a few years, my father was invited by Dhakeshwari Cotton Mills in Bangladesh to a higher position. He used to remain very busy with his work at Dhaka. So, he sent us to the village home. I, my mother and brothers were sent back to our village home at Austagram, Bangladesh. It was a very different life compared to that of Barrackpore, Kolkata.

I was born and grew up in the village during my early childhood. But, when my father got the job as a Spinning Master at Kolkata, he took us with him for a while. I was very young when we shifted to Kolkata. I do not have much recall of that period in the village. After spending some time at my father's Kolkata quarters when I came back to the village, I was more mature and rediscovered village life. It was an entirely new experience.

2

Village Life

Since in those days, there were no maternity hospitals in villages, all of us were born at home. Of course, I cannot speak about my own birth, but I have seen my younger brothers and sisters born at our home. Just before the delivery, a makeshift thatched room made of hay would be created at the remote corner of the courtyard.

The expectant mother would be accommodated in that room till the child was born. After few days of worry and trepidation a child would be born. The delivery operations would be conducted by the village midwives who were experts. There were no doctors. There was a homeopath, Dr. Chakraborty who lived in our village. He was the only savior in case of any illness. I have seen an occasion where one of my cousins, Barada's son dying. The child was very ill. The homeopath came. He checked the pulse and gave a liquid dose. The child shuddered and then he was gone. I felt very sad. When we went to live with my father at Barrackpore, near Kolkata, I was too young to remember my pre-Barrackpore village days. But when we came back, I was comparatively mature and could feel the tragedy.

Anyway, now we were back in our village again. I found that village life was slow and easy. We were many brothers and sisters including cousins in the family. The house was a sprawling one. As you entered the house, you would see a big courtyard. On the west side of the courtyard, there was a big tinned-roof house known as the Outer House. This was the meeting room of my elder uncle (Jethamasay), Jogesh Babu (Sir) with villagers and outsiders. He was my father's elder cousin brother and was considered the head of the family. His main job was to look after the family and property including farms. Although he was a very reserved person, he used to like me a lot. He had many pastimes—fishing, hunting etc. After the Outer House, you would find another tinned-roof house, just opposite to the Outer House on the east side where Jogesh Babu and his wife used to live. In fact, all the apartments in our house were made of tinned roofs. Poor people's huts in the village were made of hay. But all of our apartments were tin roofed. To the east of Jogesh Babu's apartment, we had the inner courtyard. This was as big as the outer courtyard. Our elder cousin brothers and their young village friends used to play football in the outer courtyard using soft Batapi Lebu (Grapefruit) as balls. The inner courtyard was the main action area of the family particularly the ladies where they would spend time together. To the north of Jogesh Babu's room, there was the family temple, a small tinned-roof house. This was the main activity area of my grandmother.

My grandmother was the eldest in the family and was the person responsible for all House Prayer activity. When she got married, she was only 11 years old and Jogesh Babu was 4 years old. In his younger days, Jogesh Babu was looked after by her as he lost his mother when he was very young. So, he used to hold my grandmother in great esteem. The house deity was Lord Shiva. My grandmother would offer flowers, fruits etc. in the daytime and in the evening, she used to put the Lord to sleep. She had a respectful personality but could not read or write. However, she was very knowledgeable and used to tell us stories about various Indian Gods and Goddesses. Often, she used to give me a book of the Ramayana to read. It was in poetry form. Perhaps, the book was given to her by my grandfather. Since she was not literate, she would often request me to read a part of the Ramayana which I would recite to her. Today, the Shiva idol of my grandmother is being kept at our family home at Agartala. It is now more than a hundred years old. The idol has since been installed at the small temple room of my cousin, Basudeb. He is one of the sons of my uncle, Barada and stays at Agartala. We bought this home when we migrated from our village in Bangladesh. This house at Agartala has now become our new family home.

The inner courtyard at our village home mentioned before had three living spaces on three sides. As I said the west side apartment belonged to Jogesh Babu and his wife. The apartment on the north side was allotted to my father. My mother used to stay alone there with my brothers and sisters as my father used to work at Dhaka. To the south of the inner courtyard, there was a house allotted to my uncle, Barada. But he used to live at Kushtia along with Mahendra Babu where he used to work as a sub-agent of clothes from Mohini Mills. He used to come home only during the Durga Puja holidays. So, my Aunty Manorama (Barada's wife) used to live in that portion of the house in the south side along with her children and my grandmother.

On the east side, there was a big, two-story building with three rooms on the ground floor. The south side room of that building was allotted to my other uncle Bijoy Babu and his wife. He was one of my father's cousins like Jogesh Babu. The north side room of that building was occupied by my elder cousins, Jogesh Babu's sons and daughters and the middle room was allotted to me. I used to only sleep there at night. My room was amply decorated. It was the meeting room for the important family guests from outside. It had a fancy cot and a large decorated steel trunk. On those days, people used to store money and jewelry in such large steel trunks/chests, as if these were bank lockers. People used to say that my father could tie the large steel trunk with ropes and lift it with his teeth. It must have been at least thirty kilos in weight. The room was decorated with nice frescos on all the upper side walls, painted by a local artist known as Premchand. I knew this because whenever an important family friend or guest would come, he would be served tea and sweets there and this fact would be mentioned.

The upper floor of the building was made of wood and the roof was made of tin. The whole space under the tinned-roof was without windows and very stuffy. Normally, this big room upstairs was being used as a store house for odd things. It was also used to ripen fruits like mangoes, jackfruits etc. plucked from our large orchard. The building had some grand staircases up to the inner courtyard. All of our young brothers and sisters would sit there in the morning for chitchat and brush our teeth with sticks made from small and tender neem tree branches before breakfast. On the back side of the building facing the east, there was another set of magnificent staircases where we would sit for chitchat in late morning after breakfast or in the late afternoon before sunset.

On the north side of my mother's room, there was a small kitchen garden. I used to cultivate various vegetables there. It was wonderful to see how a small tree grows from seeds. It was really astonishing to see how a seed expresses itself first as a small tree and later provides live vegetables for us and then dies on its own.

There were three large water tanks or ponds around the house. The inner tank on the south side was about 100 meters by 50 meters. It was a large one where the children used to bathe and the seniors used to catch fish. The water was very clean and the pond was very deep. We used to take water from this tank for our drinking purpose. The water would be purified by *fitkiri* (alum) and *Karpur* (camphor). There were large carps in the pond. It was a wonderful experience when the senior cousins would catch a large fish. The larger the fish the longer the time required to tame it. As a large fish would bite the food material tied to a warped steel fork, it would try to escape and would try to drag it to the deeper part of the pond. My cousins would release the string from the wheel and would let the fish go as far as it could. Later, when the fish would get tired, it would be reeled in and brought ashore by wheeling back the string and some of us, the youngsters would catch the fish with our hands as it came closer to the bank. The fish could weigh anywhere from 2 kg to 5 kg. Then the fish would be used for a feast for the family. The inner water tank had beautiful shores with palm and coconut trees on all the four sides. In the midday in summer times, sometimes, you would hear the sound of palms falling into the water—Jhoop, Jhoop, Jhoop. The children would run to the pond and pick up the palms. These were used to make special palm cakes.

On the east side of the inner water tank was a big orchard. At the eastern boundary of the orchard, there was a wild green area where there used to be wasps, butterflies, dragonflies etc. Sometimes, the young children like us would try to catch the wasps and dragonflies, not realizing how much we were hurting them. Towards the east side of the building, there was another pond. But it was muddy and covered with water lilies. This, pond was home to special types of fishes like, *Shing, Magur* and *Leta*. These fishes grow in muddy waters. We never ate those dark coloured fishes thinking that the water was dirty, muddy and soggy and these were unhygienic. The fish from this pond were normally consumed by our poor neighbors. As Mahendra Babu rose in stature, he used to send more and more money for household expenses. My elder uncle Jogesh Babu would save money from that kitty and buy all the property adjoining our main living quarters. Most of the owners of these properties were poor neighbours. One such person was Sundar Ali. We bought from him a large garden where there were a lot of banana trees on the four sides of the plot. We used to call this property, Sundar Ali's *Bagan* (Garden). We also used to cultivate *Baigan* or Big Brinjal there. This property was outside our outhouse and away from the main family house. There was a narrow public path between our main house and Sundar Ali's *Bagan*. Altogether, we had about eight acres of land including ponds, orchards, courtyards etc., enough for all of us to enjoy a comfortable village life.

Uncle Jogesh Babu had many pastimes. Being the head of the family, of course, he had to supervise the farms and the many domestic animals that we had including cows, goats, ducks, dogs etc. We had a retinue of servants and farm workers to manage the farms and livestocks.

One of Jogesh Babu's pastimes was fishing in the river. He also used to go bird hunting on the river shores. Normally, he used to go fishing late at night. He used a pointed powerful Petro-Max covered on the three sides by masks to light up the paddy field. This is why this pastime was called Alo or Light. On full moon days, at midnight, he would go fishing in the river. One boatman would steer the boat very slowly within the paddy fields. In Bangladesh, paddy fields used to get inundated by river water in the rainy season. The higher the water level rose, paddy grasses would grow faster and the paddy seeds would remain above water. This was where the big fish would go for food (algae) from the paddy. His boatman would station the boat silently at one place and both of them would keep quiet and wait. Then, suddenly the paddy field would show some turbulence due to the fish passing through. The fishes used to come in schools. Jogesh Babu would throw a spike with multiple arrows at the front end at the school of fish and one big fish would get hurt by the spike and the fish would start writhing in pain and get more and more entangled in the paddy grass and the spike.

After struggling for a while, the fish would lose strength and stop wriggling. Slowly Jogesh Babu would move closer and catch the fish with both hands. The water used to be knee-deep only. He would return home with his bounty before dawn and go to sleep. The fishes would be kept hanging on ropes at the outhouse. Whenever, Jogesh Babu would go to catch fish at night, early next morning we, the small children, would go to the outhouse very early to find out how many fishes he had caught the night before. Generally, it used to be 10/12 carp of 4/5 kg weight each. On those days, there were no freezers. So, we used to have big feasts for a few days and also distribute the extra fish to our neighbors.

He had a gun with which he used to hunt birds. Near the river shores, there used to be various types of shrubs. In the early morning, different types of multi-coloured river birds used to sit on those shrubs hunting for food, mainly small fishes. Jogesh Babu would camouflage himself with tree leaves and would shoot the birds catching them by surprise. Multiple shots would be fired and 10/12 birds would fall flat on the shrubs.

ALO; One of Jogesh Babu's past times

I remember on one occasion he allowed me to accompany him. After he fired the shot, he asked me to get down from the boat and catch the birds. It was knee-deep muddy water. I almost fainted with the loud sound of the gun. Anyway, I got down in a half-sleepy manner from the boat and caught 4/5 birds from which blood was oozing out. It was a ghastly scene. That was my first- and last-time going for bird hunting.

I was weak and thin, but I used to admire strong boys and wanted to be a football player like my father. My father used to play in the full back position and was well-known as a good player. Village boys used to play football on the river shores in the afternoons. My parents would never allow me to play with them as I might get hurt. One day, I went there without permission from my parents.

The boys allowed me to play as a centre-forward player on one of the sides. The boy from the other side was strong and stout, much older than me with very strong muscles. I had taken the ball almost to the goal post. The guy was playing in the full back position. He snatched the ball from me and was approaching our side. I charged into him directly with all my force. The result was that I was thrown 10 feet away along with the ball and broke my leg. They took me home. My father commented that I was not worthy of playing football. Anyway, that was the end of my football career.

That was the period before India obtained freedom. I made a pretend army with my younger brothers and sisters. I would wield a stick and lead the mini march saying, left, right, go front and halt. Sometimes, we used to chant "*Vande Mataram*", the patriotic song from Bankim Chandra's book Ananda Math. My mother had all the books of Bankim Chandra and a few books of Sarat Chandra. We were not supposed to read those books as we were very young. I used to hide the books beneath my reading books. I used to get absorbed in those books, particularly those depicting romance. The moment someone senior would come into my room, I would loudly start reading the text books. I was particularly in love with Ananda Math of Bankim Chandra. This was how I developed a love for Bengali literature.

One of the well-known persons from paschim gram (west part of our village) was a Congress leader. He used to be in charge of the education department at the Congress party. I remember once he visited our village and came to the eastern part of the village where we used to live. There was an *akhaada* (Gym) for the village youngsters for games and physical exercise. We also had a small community temple there. The *akhaada* had a big pond. The congress leader from paschim gram came to demonstrate to us that all of us were equal. None were of low caste. All the people should be treated as equal irrespective of colour, caste or creed as if they were our own. There was a low caste shoe-maker (*Chamar*) in the village. He was invited. He brought water from the *akhaada* pond in a pitcher and served all of us a glass of water to drink symbolizing that he was not an untouchable and we were all the same. To me, it all seemed rational and I drank the water. After I came home and my grandma heard about the episode. It was late evening. She asked me to take a bath at the pond. The next day she organized a Narayan (Lord Vishnu) Puja. I was asked to drink panchagabbi (a mixture of milk, curd, cow dung, ghee i.e., purified butter and cow-urine) to purify myself. I wondered how deep this sense of untouchability was in our society.

This was my village life and I enjoyed every moment of that time.

3

School, Family and Friends

In the early years, I never went to school as the school was 4 kilometers away and I was weak and quite lean. I was being taught at home by my uncle, Bijoy Babu. He used to work at a cotton mill in Dhaka. Suddenly he fell ill with a neurological disease. He lost strength in his legs and had to return home. He was an educated person in the house with nothing to do. So, he was assigned the task of tutoring all the children in the house. He used to teach me at his room. My father believed that just having knowledge of English, Bengali and Math was enough education. Bijoy Babu used to teach me only these subjects. As a result, even in later life, I did not give much emphasis on subjects like history, geography etc. No wonder, I just scraped through geography in my matriculation examination (school final board examination after the 10th class).

In spite of no previous formal schooling, I was admitted in the 4th class at the village high school at the age of 7. My father thought I should pass the matriculation examination by the age of 14. I never managed to sit for the final examination in class 4 as I fell ill due to typhoid. So, I had to finish school at the age of 15 instead of 14.

Our school was 4 kilometers away from our home. It was in the western part of the village. I had to walk the full distance along with other students from our locality. It was not a problem. We could walk a lot on those days. I used to love the school as we had good teachers.

I used to particularly like the mathematics teacher, Paresh Babu. His way of teaching was very good. I used to especially like his classes on factorization during the 8th grade. To me, the Math Teacher, Paresh Babu was great. Math is a subject disliked by many including myself. Paresh Babu used to teach Algebra in the 8th class. His method of teaching was liked by us all. I loved it so much that even at home, I would solve factorization problems. Unfortunately, in 1950, he was killed by some local persons during Hindu-Muslim ethnic riots and we missed him.

Austagram was a large village. It consisted of 8 small villages. “Austa” means eight. That is how the name Austagram was derived. It was the second largest village in Bangladesh, the largest being Baniachong in Sylhet district. We were from the eastern part of the village. The high school was in the western part. Going to school 4 kilometers away was fun. A number of students from purbagram, meaning eastern village, used to go together. The road was narrow with a number of troughs and valleys overlooking paddy fields. In harvest times, these paddy fields looked brilliant with ripe golden paddy in the field.

The scene was very different during the rainy season. In that season, most of the village used to remain submerged in water. We had to go to school by boat. One day, our boat capsized. We swam across to the dry land and were looking for shelter as all of us had wet clothes and wet books. We found a well-built and attractive house nearby and took shelter there. The lady of the house was very kind. She gave us dry clothes to borrow and wear and let our own clothes to get dry. She also offered us puffed rice (Muri). Later on, we learnt that the house belonged to the local dacoit. I realized that even dacoits could be nice to strangers in trouble.

Once, the school organised a theatre for the students to perform. The authorities invited the local District Magistrate who was a white Britisher. I thoroughly enjoyed the show. This was the first theatre show in my life. It seemed like a dream as if I was in a different world.

One of my best friends in the class was a Muslim boy, Aziz Ahmed. One day, he took me to a solitary place near the school. There were a few old and broken buildings. Amidst large and old trees within the middle of a semi-dense forest, the scene appeared ghostly. There was a thick, muddy pond covered with moss on which you could walk. Of course, there was water beneath and you had to balance yourself as you slowly walked. There was a unused old mosque nearby. He took me inside the mosque and asked me to recite some Arabic words. I did so and he said that I had become a Muslim. Back home, I narrated the entire episode to my grandma. I told her that I was now a Muslim. She heard the entire story and advised that I should take my clothes off and take a thorough bath in the pond as I had done when I had to purify myself after drinking water from a low caste shoemaker (*Chamar*). The next day, she organized a Narayan (Lord Vishnu, one of the important Hindu gods) *puja* (worship) as before. At the end of the puja, I was given a sip of panchagabbi (a concoction of milk, curd, cow dung, cow urine and purified butter) and I was declared a Hindu again by the priest.

In the meantime, our family earnings decreased. One day, I found that our family had been divided into two parts. One part consisted of my father and uncle Barada and the rest comprised of Jogesh Babu and Bijoy Babu. After the family division, the main kitchen went to Jogesh Babu's side. So, we used to cook food at my grandma's vegetarian kitchen. We made a make-shift small thatched roof-room for cooking our non-vegetarian food.

So far, all the money had been kept and managed by Jogesh Babu as he was the head of the family. Now, our portion had to be managed by my grandmother as she was the eldest from our side. The rest of us on our side were ladies and children. She had no money. So, she asked me to meet the local *zamindar* (Landlord), Nani Mazumdar and ask him to lend us ₹ 200.00 in cash. He was good enough to lend us ₹ 200.00 which must have been a lot of money at that time.

He knew my father and uncle well and had great regard for them. He asked me not to worry and to come again if we needed more money. He said that he would recover the money later from my father. That was a great relief.

Bangladesh was a river-centric country. Our river, Maksha, was three miles away from our house. My father was a disciplinarian. His dictum was "Early to bed and early to rise makes a man healthy, wealthy and wise". So, my father would wake me up at 5 am. I had to walk to the river alone and wash my face with river water and get back by 6 am. My father would meet me half way to check whether I had really touched the river water by looking at my washed face i.e., he would check whether I had really gone all the way or conned him by coming back from half the way.

There was a Jam (Black Plum) tree on the way at which a villager had committed suicide by hanging some days ago. The tree had some raised roots. Whenever, I used to pass that tree, I used to chant Lord Rama's (another name of Vishnu God) name and pass the place hurriedly. One day as I was passing by that tree, I tripped over the raised roots and fell to the ground. Suddenly, I felt some sensation in my ear. I felt as if the ghost of the dead man was pulling me by the ear. Out of fear, I did not dare to look up at him. After sometime, I picked up some courage and looked up. I found that it was none other than my father in a long overcoat as if he was the detective, Sherlock Holmes. He commented, "What a fool you are! You can't even walk the straight path?" I praised Lord Rama that at least, it was not a real ghost but my father.

I remember another episode. Sometimes, the village boys used to go fishing at the river shore. They used to walk down in knee-deep water with a fishing stick. They were using some worms as bait for the fish. Once when my father went out of the village on business, my mother allowed me to accompany a group of boys to go fishing. Like them, I walked down to the knee-deep water near the shore with my fishing stick and tried my luck. All the other boys who went with me caught a lot of fish. But no fish came to swallow my bent needle with the worm. I do not know why. I had to come back empty handed. Since, I was not used to staying in knee-deep water for three/four hours at a time, I came back with high fever. After that I abandoned my dreams of catching fish at the river forever.

I remember another incident. Our family went for a joy ride on the river in the evening during full moon. It was a large decorated boat (Bajra). All the members of the family were present. We spent hours together on the river, of course always staying near the shores, away from the strong waves of the mid-river. That was a fantastic experience. Only rich people used to enjoy a Bajra ride at full moon in those days. We were lucky.

It was a different experience when we used to travel long distances by boat. My mother used to go to her parents' house once in a year. My maternal uncle's house was in a distant village, called Kaligachha. We used to live in Mymensingh district. Kaligachha was in a different district called Tripura. There were no cars or trains from Mymensingh to Tripura on those days. The only way was to go by boat. That could only be done in the rainy seasons.

During the rainy season, most of the villages used to get inundated by rain water. Villages used to look like small islands. So, villages were accessible only by boat at that time. In other seasons, one had to walk long distances on foot which was not easy for women folk or children. During the rainy season, the main rivers would get connected via canals up to the villages. Via these canals, you could go almost up to the individual's house. The rivers used to be in full spate in the rainy season. There used to be big waves at the middle of the rivers where the water was very deep. Sometimes it could be treacherous and the boat could capsize in the middle of the river.

Once on the way to my maternal uncle's house, we found ourselves in a dangerous situation. We were at the middle of the river and a sudden big storm came. The boat was rocking up and down with the waves. We were almost on the verge of getting capsized. All of us were praying to God loudly—"God, save us, save us." The boatmen were trying with all their might to keep the boat steady. After a few minutes, they managed to steer the boat away from the middle to the side where the river was calmer and we were saved.

Bajra Ride with Full Family

Usually, we used to go to my maternal uncles' house when the uncles too were visiting home from their place of work. One of my uncles, Gopen Babu used to work at Tata Steel, Jamshedpur. He was a well-to-do person. One year, he was at the village home when we went to their house for holidays. One day, I went to the local market with him. Back in our village, we used to have a lot of big carps at home either from our large water pond caught by our cousins or from the river caught by Jogesh Babu. On that occasion, I noticed that my uncle was passing by many fish-sellers with big carps. He avoided them and bought some small fishes instead. I wondered why he was reluctant to buy large carps. Was he trying to save money? I received no answer.

There were no children in my maternal uncle's house at that time. So, I used to play by myself. I used to make small homes with bits of wood etc. and pretend to be a grocer. I was both the buyer and the seller. Small size stone chips were used as money for exchange. In one of the neighbour's houses there were a few girls who used to sing Tagore songs. My mother used go to their house sometimes and used to sing Tagore songs along with them using the harmonium as an accompaniment. She was not a great singer but she used to sing when she was with other singers.

My mother's elder sister was married to someone from the same village. Her husband, Nripen Babu was a revered priest in the village. We used to meet them often. Kaligachha was an affluent village. One of the rich businessmen, Mr. Saha had just started a cinema hall, the first cinema hall in the area. For the inaugural show, he invited my maternal uncle, Nripen Babu. I do not know why Nripen Babu took me along with him for the inaugural show. He held my hand and both of us sat in the first row. In those days, cinema used to be silent. You had to understand the meaning from their acting itself. The name of the play was *Mane Na Mana* (My mind does not agree). I thoroughly enjoyed the first silent cinema show in my life.

The village had a High School. It was made with red bricks and had a beautiful round pool in front of the school. The water was crystal clear and the landscape was beautiful. The promoter of the school was a local businessman known as Chakraborty. The family was known to my mother. One day, we went to visit the family. All the ladies of the house were fair and beautiful. My mother said, "Look! The ladies of the house look like Goddess Durga". I agreed. Many years later, we became a part of that family when my wife's cousin sister Manju was married to one of the sons from the family, Yogabrata. He was a student at my college, MBB (Maharaja Bir Bikram) College, Agartala.

Later we became good friends after his marriage.

There was a river trip to my mother's parental village which I vividly remember.

Like my mother, my aunts also used to go to their parental houses every year. Once I accompanied my aunt Manorama, Barada's wife, to her parent's house. One senior male had to accompany them for safety. The boats were hired boats. When my father came to the village after leaving his textile job, he used to accompany the ladies to their parental houses as other male members were working in towns. Wives of younger brothers were not allowed to talk to the elder brother-in-law directly. So, I had to accompany them so that they could exchange information between my father and my aunts, using me as the medium. Aunt Manorama had an elder sister who used to live on the way to her native village. It was a small town called Habiganj. Our boat made the first stop at Habiganj. As soon we landed ashore, a motor car went by us making a loud noise and constantly blowing a horn. That was the first time, I had ever seen a motor car.

Aunt Manorama grew up with her father at Shillong, a small town in Assam (now, it has become a separate state, Meghalaya). She used to wear shoes at Shillong. Generally, in our village, children used to walk barefoot and had no shoes. I had no shoes. Aunt Manorama insisted that I must buy a pair of sandals before I go to her sister's home. So, on the way to their house, my father bought a pair of shoes for me. These were my first pair of sandals in life. I walked a little distance but got blisters on my feet. So, instead of wearing the sandals, I carried them with me as precious items. I even slept with those in my arms as I was worried that someone might take away my sandals while I was sleeping.

We stayed there for a couple of days. My aunt's brother-in-law had a sweet shop. So, we used to have tasty sweets like *Rasagolla, Pantua* etc. every day. After a couple of days at Habigunj, we resumed our journey by boat to my aunt's parental village, Baniachong. By late evening, we reached their village. But we could not locate the exact house. It was pitch dark, with no light, no person anywhere. It was a marshy area with a lot of trees and shrubs. So, we kept the boat near the shore and slept on the boat itself. When we woke up the next morning, we realised that we had already reached their house. In the early morning a maid from their house came to collect water and spotted us. We were welcomed to the house. Unfortunately, in the boat, I had been badly bitten by mosquitoes in that marshy water and I caught Malaria. I was not allowed to take any solid food. I felt very bad that all of them were having delicious meals while I was being served with only tasteless barley and bitter quinine pills to cure Malaria. That was a bad experience.

Another time, I went with my other aunt, Bijoy Babu's wife, Renu to their village. The people there were well-to-do and educated. Unlike Baniachong or Austagram with tinned-roof houses, there were a lot of houses made of bricks. I saw a small brick-made house a little away from the main house. I thought it could not be a house to live in but must be a small temple. When I asked a person which God was in that temple, I was astonished to hear that it was a brick-made toilet. I had seen that all toilets in villages were normally made of hay, bamboo and tin. I realized how rich the village was.

The western part (Pashchim gram) of our village was a Muslim dominated area whereas our part i.e., eastern part (Purba gram) was a Hindu dominated area. We had never felt any religious difference. We were quite friendly with each other in spite of the religious difference. Often, I used to visit our Muslim labourers at their village homes. I would often share a bowl of puffed rice with them. Although India was partitioned on religious lines into India and Pakistan in 1947, we had stayed in our village home in Pakistan even after partition as we still felt safe and comfortable. After partition, many Hindus started to leave for India as they were being victimized in jobs and other opportunities. Our family was still staying at the village home as we never felt threatened.

During the 1950 Hindu-Muslim ethnic riots, it so happened that the only daughter of our math teacher, Paresh Babu came from Kolkata to visit her parents. One night some hooligans attacked the family in the dead of night. They butchered her in her bed room. Her little child was also stabbed with a knife. Old Paresh Babu's body was sliced into three pieces. This incident with our teacher shook our family. On hearing this ghastly news, my grandma decided to leave the village and move to India. This was the end of my early school life and growing up in the village.

4

Father's Business Life

Being independent in nature, my father used to have differences of opinion with his British bosses at work. So, he left his job at Dhakeswari Mills and decided to start a business instead. After leaving the job at Dhakeswari Mills, my father came to stay with us in our village permanently and started his career in business. He would start with one, fail and then restart with another. Unfortunately, every business that he started, failed.

I remember his first business. He started a grocery shop in the village. While my father used to manage the business through his people in the front of the shop, I had to take my books and study at the back of the shop. My father was a body builder and had a robust build whereas I was a lean fellow like my mother, without much physical strength. He would ask me to do some physical exercise at the anteroom of the shop, which I used to do very reluctantly. Of course, now, I realize those forced exercises helped me to develop physically later in life.

I remember an incident at that time. One day I was returning home from my father's shop. I was walking briskly. From the opposite side two village boys were coming. By accident, one of my hands touched the shirt pocket of one of the boys. Perhaps, a few coins were in his pocket and it made a jinggling sound. He shouted at me and accused me of being a thief. I did not know what to do. His companion told him, "Do you know who he is? He is Ranada Babu's son. He would never do something like that" and I was let off. I realized then that I belonged to a respectable family.

My Parents

My father had a number of friends in the village and he had very little interest in business. He used to pass time with them. After a period of time, his grocery business failed. He would not go back to any job either. So, he started and failed in many other businesses one after another. One such business was a wholesale business in paddy. He used to send paddy by boat to distant places. He was good in sales but not in collecting the payments. He was friendly with the buyers and would give them credit. Over time, many defaulted. So, he lost this business too. Then, he started selling pearls. He used to bring a large number of raw pearls from which we had to select the beautiful ones. He would sell the assorted and choicest pearls to goldsmiths at a higher price. This also failed though I did not know why.

At the time, India was partitioned, my father acquired some forest land in North Bengal on lease and he used to supply wood from the forest to Calcutta. He used to stay alone at Siliguri and was running the business while we stayed at our village.

My uncle was doing well as a sub-agent of Mohini Mills. He had a good business sense and used to earn a reasonable amounts of money. He was devoted to his elder brother. Every time my father lost money in his business my uncle would refinance him again to start another business.

At the time when our teacher, Paresh Babu was killed at the village, my father's business of supplying wood from North Bengal to Kolkata was apparently doing well. He used to take a forest land on lease from the Govt. through auction, get timber out of these forests and supply timber to wood dealers at Kolkata. My grandmother sent an urgent telegram to my father to immediately rush home. He left the sprawling business in north Bengal to one of our village neighbour's sons, Tarani Biswas to take care. He usurped the business and absconded with all the money. That was the end of my father's forest leasing business.

5

The Partition

In 1947, India attained freedom from British rule after a long struggle. But the British cleverly divided united India into two parts, India and Pakistan.

The establishment of partition was based on religion. Before partition, Indians had formed a political party called Congress in which both Hindus and Muslims were members.

There was never any question of a Hindu-Muslim divide. When the British realized that they would have to give in to the demand for freedom to Indians anyway, they thought of dividing the Indian society on religious lines perhaps to ensure that the Indians remained weak. They encouraged a well-known practicing Muslim lawyer from the UK, Mr. Mohammed Ali Jinnah to come back to India and give political leadership to the Muslims.

Jinnah thought this was an opportunity to wield power and formed a political party called the "Muslim League" whose avowed objective was to demand a separate land for Indian Muslims. Ultimately, India was divided into two parts India and Pakistan. Muslim majority areas went to Pakistan. The rest remained as India.

The leaders from the Indian side, mainly the leaders like Gandhi and Nehru declared that India would remain a secular country where people of all faiths, be they Hindus or Muslims, Christians, Sikhs or Jains would have equal rights.

Bangladesh was a Muslim dominated area situated in the eastern part of Undivided India where we had lived for generations. It came to be known as East Pakistan. The other Muslim dominated area was in the western part of India. That part became known as West Pakistan. So, geographically, Pakistan was a combination of two states with the Indian State in the middle, and with no commonality amongst the people on either side except religion. They spoke different languages and were poles apart in community norms. Not only were they divided physically and linguistically, there was no similarity in social practices.

Actually, Bengal was one state in British times. The Bengali Hindus were talented and educated and undivided Bengal was the hub of the anti-British agitation. So, the British divided Bengal into two parts in 1905; the Muslim majority part came to be known as East Bengal and the Hindu-majority part came to be known as West Bengal. That was the first time the British drove a wedge between Hindus and Muslims in India. Unfortunately for us, the East Bengal part became East Pakistan during the partition of India. We were still living in East Pakistan (now known as Bangladesh) as if nothing had happened. As I said, Pakistan was declared as a theological country based on Islam as the official religion in 1947. We were Hindus and not very much wanted in the new dispensation. There was discrimination in jobs and elsewhere. Still, we used to live at our village since we had good relations with everybody, irrespective of religion. We felt safe in Bangladesh where our family had been living for hundreds of years.

There was more commonality of culture between the people of East Pakistan and West Bengal than between East and West Pakistan. Eventually, there were fights between the Urdu Speaking West Pakistanis and Bengali speaking East Pakistanis. Ultimately, East Pakistanis acquired freedom from the dominant West Pakistan under a visionary leader, Sheikh Mujibur Rahman with some help from neighbouring India. They called their new country, Bangladesh. So, undivided India was now divided into three parts—Pakistan, Bangladesh and the rest of undivided India remained as

India. As I said, India declared itself as a secular state under the influence of Gandhi, Nehru and Netaji Bose although these were predominantly Hindu dominated areas.

I remember the tragic situation when we left our house at Austagram, Bangladesh leaving all our properties and valuables behind. Overnight we hurriedly packed some essential clothes and migrated to the nearby border town of Agartala in Indian territory. The year was 1950. Agartala was the capital of the nearest Indian state, known as Tripura. Passports were not in place then. So, legally, there was no barrier to migrate. I remember, we first left our village by boat and boarded a train from a place called Brahmanbaria at night and stayed at the border town called Akhaura and took shelter in the house of a Hindu family for the night. In the early morning, we went to the Akhaura-Agartala border to cross over to India.

It was a terrible scene. Thousands of Hindu migrants like us were struggling to enter India simultaneously. East Pakistan (now Bangladesh) was a very new country then and it did not have proper border police or controls. There were some paramilitary police on guard who had no formal dress. They used to wear only a badge on their shirt. They were called Ansars.

Amongst the milieu, I remember they were beating youngsters like us, although lightly, to keep the queue in proper order and avoid chaos. I was 13 years old then. Ultimately, after much struggle, we reached Agartala at 4 pm. It was a small hilly border town in north east India. We went to Agartala as we had a cousin there. My cousin did not have a proper house to stay. So, he took us to one of our distant relatives, Nalini Chakraborty. His house was on a small hill top. He was himself a poor migrant. But he offered us rice and dried fish (*sutki*). After a long day of fear, helplessness and hunger, it tasted delightful.

Part-II

Life after Bangladesh

Akhaura Junction

6

Agartala Days

We stayed in the house of our host, Nalini Chakraborty for a few days till we found a rented place for ourselves. At our village home at Bangladesh, we used to use kerosene lamps at night for lighting. As a result, we always preferred to read in the clear morning daylight. At our rented house, it was for the first time, we had the experience of reading under bright electric light. Everything appeared bright and clear. It was a treat to read books at night.

After we went to our rented home, we applied to receive money from the Govt. This was relief money for migrants from Bangladesh. Although we did not stay at Govt. shelters, we were considered as migrants from Bangladesh and eligible for relief money. Our family used to receive ₹ 10 per week as relief. Every week on Mondays, I used to join the queue in the morning and return home with the money in the evening.

I remember one episode. I started from home at 10 am. There was a long queue of around 500 people. Most of the people in the queue lived in temporary refugee shelters provided by the government. We were staying in a comfortable rented home while others were poor people living in shabby Govt. shelters. I used to feel a little uneasy standing in queue with all of them.

On that day, the officials started distributing money from 2 pm. onwards. After receiving the money, I reached home on foot by around 6 pm, fully exhausted. My uncle, Barada asked me whether I had eaten anything during the day. I said no as I did not have any money with me. He said you had 10 rupees relief money with you. Why did you not buy some sweets and eat on the way back? I said that I did not think it was right for me to spend the money on myself which was meant for the entire family.

Anyway, soon my father bought a lorry with the money provided by my uncle, Barada. This time, my father started a transport business. We removed ourselves from the refugee list. I was happy to be relieved of the usual duty of standing in queue for long hours for such a small amount of dole.

As the eldest boy in the family, I had to do the shopping for the family. We came to know that there was an open bazaar (market) on the India-Bangladesh border where Bangladeshi villagers used to bring fresh vegetables, fish etc. to sell. The transaction used to take place at a no man's land at the open border between the two countries. The sellers used to accept Indian money as Indian money was more valuable to them than Bangladeshi Taka. Agartala was the capital of the Indian state of Tripura. It was a hilly place with not much vegetation. So, getting fresh things from Bangladesh was a boon. I remember one event. One day, I bought a tortoise and brought this hanging on my hand tied by a string. We used to eat tortoise meat. It was cheaper than goat meat. Being tired of holding the tortoise on one hand for a long time, I tried to change my hands and tried to take the tortoise by the other hand. In the process, I was a bit unmindful and the tortoise bit one of my fingers. I did not buy any tortoise thereafter.

Being in the middle of the school session, I was unable to get admission at any good school. I was admitted to a school which was started by Hindu refugee teachers from Bangladesh. It was a makeshift shelter made of bamboo and hay. The teachers who came from Bangladesh during the ethnic riots at Bangladesh took this initiative. They were from various political leanings. Some were Congressmen belonging to the Nehru-Gandhi group, some were communists belonging to the Jyoti Basu group while some were socialists. They used to fight amongst each other on political issues.

Almost every now and then, some group or other purportedly used to start a fire in our makeshift school. Our main job as students was to remain ready to douse the fire with buckets of water obtained from the campus pond. We had neither any proper library at that time nor could we buy books as most of us were refugees and could not afford to buy books.

So, our mind was not too focused on studies but just on survival. I took admission in Class Eight but the pre-final examination was only two months away. As I said, I did not have proper books to study. Six of us failed the term examination and decided to take our own lives. We went to a hilly place on the outskirts of the city called Kunjaban. It was near the summer palace of the erstwhile King. Having reached the place, we were contemplating about the means as to how to take our lives. Suddenly, one of us began to recite a famous poem from Nobel laureate poet Tagore, which said 'Why should I die, before I am actually dead.' All of us agreed with this view. So, we decided to drop the idea and came back home with the intent that we should study hard and pass the examination next time. So, we did. Although my marks improved thereafter, I had to be content with only a second division in the school final examination two years later. I missed the first division only by a whisker. Perhaps, if I had a proper place to study at home, and if I had some books, maybe I could have managed a better performance.

I took the help of some tutorial during the end of my school final days. I had never taken private tuition before. But, because the time left for the school final examination was very limited, my father organized a private tutor for me for about three months. We had to go to the teacher's home. A mattress would be laid on the floor and about ten of us would sit cross-legged and study together. He would ask each of us separately about his/her problem. I used to study only mathematics. I found that although all of us paid the same amount of money, it was mostly I who was asking questions and getting answers. I wondered why the other kids were wasting their parents' money and teacher's time.

One of my married cousin sisters, Parul used to live at Agartala. I used to visit their house often. Her husband was a teacher and an interesting character. I was one of his fans. Often, he would get up from his seat, walk up and down and utter, "*Kim Kartyabyam Ataparam*" This is a Sanskrit sentence. It means "What should I do next?" I really did not understand it's significance till an episode happened at our house.

My mother was a sickly person. She would be suffering from something or other all the time. Once, she had fever. In the afternoon my father asked me to bring some medicine from the nearby pharmacy. I went out to buy the medicine. I met a friend on the way. He asked me to accompany him to another friend. Later, the three of us spent some time at a roadside tea shop. As a puritan household, youngsters like us were not served tea at our home lest we become addicted. So, a cup of tea was a treat for me. I came home late at night and forgot all about my mother's medicine. On reaching home, my father asked me where was the medicine? I was shocked that I had forgotten all about it and cursed myself for the lapse. At that time, I remembered Parul's husband and promised to myself that at every step in my life, I would always ask myself, "What is my next duty?" I never forgot any urgent thing thereafter.

After the school final examination, I went for a vacation to our village home in Bangladesh where some of my uncles, aunts and cousins still used to live. Life at the village was very slow, but I was having a good time. My uncle, the elder cousin brother of my father, Jogesh Babu used to love me a lot. He used to allot big pieces of fish and the full fish head for me. I also used to get large Alphonso mangoes with milk at dinner as a special treat. I was having a gala time with the cousins and village folk. It was also a quiet time for me with neither any bother about studies nor thinking about what to do next after schooling.

But all too soon, I received a telegram from my father that I had to immediately rush back to Agartala and take admission in the local college as I had passed the school final examination and college seats were limited. On those days, there was neither any motorable road nor any railway station in our village. We had to take a steamer to reach any nearby town which had a railway connection. The steamer could not reach the shores of the river as it was shallow. So, we had to take a boat and wait at the middle of the river where we had to wait for the steamer to come. The timing of the steamer was not fixed. It used to be generally around noon time. We went to the mid-river on two consecutive days but missed the ferry as by that time it had left. The delay used to happen mainly due to the long lunch period. Jogesh Babu and my aunt, his wife would insist that I must have a sumptuous good lunch before I left home. So, I was getting late. On the third day, I insisted that I should leave immediately after breakfast and wait on the boat at the mid-river long before the steamer reached the scheduled place. I was lucky on the third day. At long last, I left the village for Agartala.

Although, by that time, there was a passport system, I had no passport and had visited Bangladesh clandestinely. While returning, I had to come via Chittagong, a town in Bangladesh where one of my uncles, Mr. Chakraborty (Grandfather Mahendra's son-in-law) used to live. He was a tea planter and used to own several tea gardens in Bangladesh, one of which was at the Bangladesh-Agartala border. I stayed at his beautiful bungalow at Chittagong for one night. In the afternoon, the male members in the family went to play football on their private football field. They used to invite other clubs from nearby tea gardens to play friendly matches with their club. They had an ambassador car. I went in the car along with them. I had never boarded a car before and did not know how to open the doors. On reaching the field, all of them got down leaving me behind. I did not know how to get out of the car and was stuck in the car. All the windows of the car were closed. So, they could not hear my cry. About 15 minutes later, they realized that I was stuck in the car and one of them came back to take me from the car. I was relieved.

The next morning, I was taken to the tea garden at the Bangladesh-Indian border. I stayed in the manager's house during the night. He was a Muslim. Those were the days of ethnic riots. So, I was apprehensive. But nothing happened and the night passed off peacefully. At home, we used to eat food on metal plates. At the manager's house they were using earthenware plates. I was not very comfortable either with the utensils or with the type of food being served for dinner. So, I did not eat much. Hence, I felt a little hungry later but somehow managed the night. In retrospect, the manager was very polite and tried to take care of me to the best of his ability.

The next morning, he sent me to the Bangladesh-India border along with one of his trusted workers. The border was a porous one with no fence. He took me to the Indian border and helped me onto a rickshaw. I felt very safe and happy to be back at home.

As soon as I reached home, I was asked by my father to get admission in the local college to study science. He never asked me whether I would prefer science, arts, or commerce. My father's word was the last decision—nobody could question or alter it.

Maharaja Bir Bikram College, Agartala

I took admission in I.Sc. (Intermediate Science) with Physics, Chemistry and Mathematics as main subjects with Biology as an elective. The local college was known as M.B.B. College (Maharaja Bir Bikram College). Maharaja Bir Bikram was a local king. All these days, I used to be lectured by my father to study well. Now things changed. After joining the college, I observed that my father was no longer asking me to study well. Perhaps, it was because he had never been to college. He had to discontinue studies after his school final. Now, I felt that it was my duty to study well. I also found interest in these science subjects, particularly physics and chemistry.

I secured first division at Intermediate Science (I.Sc.). I never thought what I should do after I.Sc. I thought that I would have to continue with B.Sc. at the same college.

After the I.Sc. result was announced, I found that many of my friends were going away to study engineering, veterinary, medicine etc. They must have applied beforehand. All of them secured lower marks than me in I.Sc. My result was much better than them in every way. But I had no knowledge of these courses and did not apply.

So, I was left behind in the college and continued with B.Sc. I took Honors in Chemistry as I had a knack for chemistry. In the meantime, a few of our professors started moving to Kolkata for better opportunities. We had only one chemistry professor left, Prof. Anil Bhattacharya. He was a good professor and I used to like him. I was the only student who took honors in Chemistry. One day, Prof. Anil Bhattacharya called me to his office and asked me to leave the 'honors' course on my own volition as it was very difficult for him to teach I.Sc., B.Sc. and 'honors' courses alone. He asked me to sign a paper to that effect that I was giving up Honors of my own volition. As an obedient student, I did so. That was the end of my 'honors' degree. I continued with the normal stream of B.Sc. without Honors. However, I did extremely well in

B.Sc. examination, and obtained Distinction with high marks in all subjects like Chemistry, Physics and even in Mathematics.

During the B.Sc. course, I found that I was quite good in academics and found a role as a kind of leader amongst the students. They used to approach me for different initiatives. I started a wallpaper along with the students. It was popular. I wrote an article on that wallpaper and gave it a caption, "All was one". I argued that everything in this universe was energy. For example, in atomic fission, one could convert matter into energy and it was understood that cosmic rays were continuously impinging on the earth's surface and earth's weight has been increasing day by day. It makes me remember Einstein's – "Unified Field Theory". I argued that all types of energy were inter-convertible. For example, electricity could be converted into heat, light, sound, etc. Thus, matter could be converted into energy and energy could be converted into matter. All types of energies were inter-convertible. So, everything in this universe was the same. I read a book, History of Science by Davy which shed a lot of light on the topic. I found great satisfaction and became confident that I could write on scientific topics.

However, I did not have such luck with literature. During my I.Sc. class, I had to study Bengali literature as well. Our professor of Bengali was Prof. Ranen Sen. He was an extremely good teacher. I used to admire him. He said that I had a knack for literature and could write. It was well-known that Bengalis are poetic by nature. There was hardly any Bengali youth who had not written one or two poems during their college days. That inspired me to write a poem on Tagore which I did. After that I picked up the courage and wrote a story and submitted it for inclusion in the College journal. The title was "*Bhul*" in Bengali, meaning "False" in English. It was about a failed love story of a young boy. When the journal was published, I looked at the content and found a story entitled "*Bhul*" had been published. I was thrilled. Soon, I realized it was not mine. The writer was different although the title of the story was the same. I never tried to be a writer thereafter.

Similarly, I had no ability in sports either. During the college cricket match, I was given the role of a batsman. I thought it would be very easy. From the opposite side, the bowler delivered the ball, but before I could even play the bat, there was a loud roar "Out". I asked what had happened. I had not even batted. They said that the wicket had already fallen. That was the end of my cricket career.

As I said I was lean and thin compared to other students. Like my mother I used to suffer from bouts of diarrhea and fever from time to time. Umakanta Academy was the best school in the town. They had a very good football field. By the side of the football field, they had kept a couple of parallel bars in an open place. I found that those students who were practicing parallel bar had good biceps. So, in the early mornings when no other students used to be there, I started practicing on the parallel bar on my own. Within six months, I found that my health was improving and I was developing reasonably good biceps. I also bought a book on Yoga and started practicing Yoga on my own. This was also a success. Thereafter, my health improved substantially.

Anyway, I passed B.Sc with distinction but did not know what to do thereafter. There was no university at Agartala on those days. So, there was no scope to study for a Master degree at Agartala. The only way left for me was to apply for a local government job as there was no industry either. My mother and aunt were of the opinion that I had done enough studies and advised me to take a job instead.

Soon, an opportunity came. The local Govt. was looking for a food inspector. I applied and appeared for the interview. The interviewer asked me the composition of blood, which obviously I could not answer.

That was the end of my job expectation at Agartala.

7

Tryst with M.Sc.

I was told by one of my professors that although I did not have an 'Honors' in Mathematics, I may get a chance to study M.Sc in Mathematics at Calcutta University without honors because my marks in Mathematics in B.Sc. was very good and there were few takers of Mathematics in M.Sc.

I could also study Chemistry at Dhaka University, in spite of no honors at B.Sc. but the problem was arrangements for expenses and getting a visa from the Pakistan government. My father said that he could not bear the expenses.

I received a scholarship of ₹ 50 per month from the Govt. of Tripura for post-graduate studies. So, I took a chance to go to Calcutta on my own and try my luck there. I still had in mind to study Chemistry if I could get a chance. One local doctor at Agartala, named Captain Nath, had one of his brothers working at the famous Indian Institution for the Cultivation of Science at Calcutta as a senior scientist. He was kind enough to give me a letter introducing me to his scientist brother. Armed with this letter, I ventured for Calcutta. While going to Calcutta, I went via Kushtia in Bangladesh where my uncle, Barada lived in the house of my grandfather, Mahendra Babu. My father gave me fifteen rupees and my uncle gave me a piece of paper called *Hawala* (Voucher) which would entitle me to get one hundred and fifty rupees on showing it to a businessman at Burrabazar in Kolkata. So, I had just one hundred and sixty-five rupees in all in my kitty. With this as asset, I took the train from Kushtia and landed at Sealdah station in Kolkata and started walking on foot to my uncle Tarak Babu's house in the late evening without giving him any prior information. My idea was to take shelter in his house and study M.Sc.

Uncle Tarak was my father's cousin. He was the son of Mahendra Chakraborty. He was a rich person by our standards. He was doing some kind of business. I remember reaching his house from Sealdah station on foot with the luggage on my head and reached at 11 pm. I was wearing boots without socks and a Bengali dhoti and a shirt, more like the famous cinema star, Uttam Kumar from Bengali cinema. Uttam Kumar would often play the role of a poor young man fresh from a village coming to Kolkata to make a fortune. It was a similar situation with me.

Reaching Uncle's House from Sealdah Station on Foot with the Luggage on My Head

When I reached my uncle's house, he could not recognize me as I had never met him before. On being asked who I was, I told him my nick name Mantu, as I was universally known in my family circle as Mantu. My aunt, Tarak Babu's wife came to my rescue. She spoke in a low voice from behind him and said that perhaps, I was one of his nephews from Agartala. I had never introduced myself to a stranger before and did not know how to introduce myself to an outsider. Even after aunt's whispering, he did not recognize me. Then, I plucked up some courage and told him my father's name, Ranada Kanta Bhattacharya. Then, very reluctantly, he recognized who I was and allowed me to step in.

I was allotted a bare wooden cot without any mattress whereas everyone in the family had proper beds. Generally, this cot was used to store extra quilts. I did not mind that as we were used to such hardships. Problem was with food. At home, we used to eat rice thrice a day. We used to eat a lot of rice. Here, I had to manage with very little rice. My aunt would give me a couple spoonsful of rice and ask "is that enough?" I had to say that "it was enough" because it would look odd in front of my cousin brothers, all of whom were happy with a couple of spoons of rice. I did not know how they managed with so little rice. I thought that the city boys consumed less food than us. As a result, I always used to remain half-full at uncle's house and felt very hungry, particularly at noon. This was more painful after I joined the university. I used to start from home by bus in the morning. There was no food in the middle till dinner at night.

Anyway, after I reached my uncle's house, the next day, I went to meet Dr. Nath (Dr. Captain Nath's brother) at the Indian Institution for the Cultivation of Science. I introduced myself and handed over Dr. Captain Nath's letter to him. He was kind and immediately spoke to Professor Rakhsit, Head of the Chemistry department at the famous Presidency College for a vacancy in M.Sc. class. He recommended me as I had very good marks in the subject. Dr. Nath said that I should go and meet Professor Rakhsit immediately as there was only one seat left and Prof. Rakshit had agreed to accommodate me. Unfortunately, this did not happen. On the opposite side of the Indian Institution for the Cultivation of Science, there was another famous Research Institution known as the Indian Institution for Glass and Ceramics. One of my chemistry professors from Agartala, Prof. Biren Sinha, a Manipuri, joined there as a researcher. I used to like him. So, I went to meet him to give him the good news that I was to get admission to the famous Presidency college. He was very happy and asked me to have tea and snacks with him to celebrate the news.

That very night, the Governor of West Bengal died, and the Government declared a three-day holiday from the next day. So, I was able to meet Professor Rakhsit only on the fourth day. When I met him, he apologized saying that someone had already taken the seat.

So, I was left with only Mathematics as an alternative to try my luck. Although I was not keen on mathematics, I approached the university the next day and managed to get a seat in Mathematics. I had neither any proper place to study at uncle's home nor did I like the subject. Anyway, I managed to get promoted to the sixth year.

I had two cousin brothers in Tarak Uncle's family. I was asked to teach them which I used to do. One evening, my uncle and aunt went out for dinner at a famous Chinese restaurant, called Peiping on Park Street. I was teaching my cousins in the evening. On that day while I was teaching them, the elder cousin commented that I was a burden to the family. I was very hurt and decided to leave then and there.

I had already been planning to leave the house anyway. I had been looking for a suitable boarding house near the university for quite a while as the distance to the university from my uncle's house was too far. One of the known persons told me that there was a vacancy at a guest house near the university, but it would cost me thirty-three rupees per month. I was dilly dallying. At that time, I was giving tuition to a student from whom I used to earn fifty rupees per month. So, I had the means to pay the guest house charges. Hence, I decided to leave my uncle's house then and there.

Uncle Tarak also used to advise me from time to time to find a place near the University. Perhaps, he wanted me to get out of his house. He would often remind me about it. By the time my uncle and aunt returned home that night after dinner at 11 pm, I was packed and ready to leave. I told him that I had found a place to stay near the university and had to leave on that night itself. I said goodbye to the family and left. My uncle said that it was an unearthly time, almost midnight. I might not get a bus so late at night. I was so hurt by my cousin's comment that I decided to leave my uncle's house that night itself. I answered that I had to go there on that night itself as otherwise the accomodation would be allotted to someone else. When I reached the main road with my luggage, luckily, I found the last bus was going. That was the end of my stay in my rich uncle's house.

At the guest house (also known as mess in the local language), there were three beds in each room adjacent to each other. The bed in the middle of one room was allotted to me. The owner of the guest house used to provide lunch and dinner, but no breakfast. One of the two persons who were my neighbours in the room used to share his breakfast with me. He used to cut his bread into three parts and one part was allotted for me. It was very kind of him. They were all working people and I was the only student in the guest house. I was managing my time reasonably well. During the spare time, I started playing table tennis at the university along with one of the M.Sc. students from Kashmir. Unfortunately, my student, taking private tuition from me passed the board examination and my tuition job was over. I was looking for another tuition. There was a gap of a month to find the new tuition. I had no money to pay the guest house owner. So, I requested one of my maternal uncles,

Gopen Bhattacharya who was a chemist at Tata Steel to lend me fifty rupees so that I could manage one month's expenses. He did so but perhaps he felt that I would be asking him money every now and then. So, he arranged an interview for me at TELCO or Tata Engineering and Locomotive Co. Ltd. (now known as Tata Motors) for the position of a chemist. On those days, I started dreaming of obtaining a M.Sc. in Math and then going for Ph.D. in nuclear physics. That was the period when the development of nuclear energy was happening in India. BARC (Bhabha Atomic Research Centre) was a research institution of national importance. I used to dream of working there.

I informed my parents that I would not go for the interview and instead continue with my studies. But uncle Barada and my father sent a telegram that I must attend the interview because it was very difficult to get a job with the prestigious Tatas. So, very reluctantly, I went for the interview. One of my roommates from the guest house, Madhusudan Babu was going to his father-in-law's place at Tata at that very time. He invited me to accompany him. So, I went with him and attended the interview. Unfortunately, I was not successful at the interview. And I was back to Kolkata to pursue my M.Sc. studies. Although I was not liking my studies in Math, I was sure that I would get at least a high second class.

Even at the guest house, I did not have much time to study as I used to spend almost three to four hours a day including bus travel for the private tuition job. I used to get tuitions mainly for the weaker students who just wanted to pass the board examination. As soon as they would pass, I had to find a new tuition. Most of my students were very average. It was easy to teach them. In my last tuition, however, I tutored a bright and meritorious student of class 10. His father was the Regional Manager of Life Insurance Corporation. It was a very prestigious job in those days. They used to stay at a famous building on Park Street known as Queens Mansion. I used to teach him only mathematics. As per my previous practice, I used to ask the student to solve 10 questions so that I could correct them later. Here, the student used to complete not only the assigned questions but would do a few more sums and used to leave one or two most difficult ones for me to solve. Instead of giving immediate solutions, I had to apply my brain and find the answers myself. One day, it so happened that I was trying to solve a knotty question and it was taking a lot of time. Suddenly, the boy's father came and said it was already 11 pm. The last bus would be leaving. I hurriedly left and caught the last bus. He was a very good student. I am sure he must have done well in life. My job there was only for three months. Once the exam was over, I was again without a private tuition job.

In the last phase of my M.Sc. studies, I managed to get an interesting part-time job as an assistant to a rich person who used to write books on Vaishnav religion. I learned from him about Vaishanavism and proof reading. He used to pay me ₹ 50 pm, enough to continue with my studies. He used to stay at Tollygunj while I used to stay at College Street which was very far away. Up and down travel by bus and work used to take almost 4 hours per day. I had to reach his place by 9.30 am. So, I had to start by 8.30 am whereas our breakfast time at the boarding was 9 am. So, I was missing my breakfast and used to feel hungry. My employer used to have a sumptuous breakfast right before my eyes but never offered me even a cup of tea. One day, he said that I had to reach his home by 9 am. I thought that this was a good opportunity to ask for breakfast. I agreed on the condition that he would provide me breakfast as I would miss my breakfast at the boarding house. He agreed. So, I started coming to his place by 9 am. Alas, instead of the sumptuous breakfast I expected, he used to offer me a cup of tea and two biscuits.

Anyway, after coming back from the unsuccessful interview at Tatas, I focused on my studies. I might have managed to get a high second class in M.Sc. as I had not studied well before. I still dreamt of a Ph.D. in nuclear physics. After about 6 months (after the interview), just before the M.Sc. final examination, there was a letter from Tata Motors that I could join the company as a chemist. Later, I came to know that they had shortlisted four candidates including me but there were only three positions then. So, they had kept me in reserve for future requirement. One of the candidates who had joined left six months after joining. Perhaps, he got a better offer from elsewhere. I was asked to join in his place. So, reluctantly, I left my studies at Calcutta University and went to join Tata Engineering and Locomotive company at Jamshedpur as a Chemist.

That was the end of my study at Calcutta University. I once watched a film called, "*Kacher Swarga*" (Broken Dream). In the movie, the story was of a medical student who could not complete his studies in medicine due to lack of money and instead took a job in a military hospital as a paramedic. Then a war took place. He was sent to the war front. It was a fierce war. There were many casualties and wounded soldiers used to be brought to the military medical centre. Because of paucity of doctors, he was asked by the authorities to perform some surgical operations. Because of his experience at the medical college as a student, he performed those operations very successfully. He thought that he might now be considered as a competent surgeon. Alas, immediately after the war he was reverted back to the position of a paramedic and his chance of being a surgeon vanished as a broken dream. I thought that my position was similar. I could not hope to become a Ph.D. in nuclear science. My dream of becoming a nuclear scientist had gone forever like that of the character in the film.

PART - III

Early Work Life

TELCO Gate in 1956

8

Life after Kolkata

I had two maternal uncles working at Tatas. Both of them were happy and advised me to join Tata Motors. I was unsure. I used to still dream of my Ph.D. Whereas the uncles were insistent that I join Tatas, both my aunts on the other hand, were on my side. They advised me to go back to the university and continue with my Ph.D. and hence there was a tussle in the family for some time.

Gates of Tata Motors

Tatas used to provide staff quarters to their employees to stay but the allocation used to take a long time as there was shortage of staff quarters. My aunts said that none of my uncles had obtained company living quarters immediately after joining. They had had to stay for many years in a nearby private colony without the many civic facilities as was available at the Tata quarters. So, the aunts gave me a condition that I should join only if the company provided staff quarters for me to stay from day one. That appeared to be an unreasonable demand from a new employee. I was sure that I would not get the staff quarters and therefore I would be able to go back and continue with my studies. I went to my future boss, Dr. U.K. Bhattacharya, a D.Sc. from the Massachusetts Institute of Technology (MIT) and gave him my proposal that I must get a place to stay from day one, otherwise I would have to decline the job. To my surprise, he agreed to my proposal. So, I became a chemist at Tata Motors.

At long last, I left my studies in the middle of sixth year and joined Tata Motors as a chemist at the age of 20, only six months before the final examination. I would have at least got a second class and become a M.Sc. I could have also tried for a Ph.D. in nuclear physics, but this was not to be.

At my time, the company was named TELCO (Tata Engineering and Locomotive Co. Limited). The company used to manufacture Locomotives, Mercedes Trucks and General Heavy Engineering items. It started a new foundry for obtaining own casting material needs and needed chemists.

I joined the Foundry division as a chemist. My job at Tata Motors was to determine the content of various elements like Silicon, Manganese, Phosphorus etc. in steel samples. But I failed as a chemist in practice although I obtained almost 90% marks in the chemistry practical examination during my B.Sc. final examination. Now, I found out that I failed as a chemist because I was colour blind. I didn't know that I was colour blind. When determining manganese in steel, I was getting a result between 45%-65% while the actual figure should have been 55%. I was not able to decide which was the right end point in titration.

Realising My Colour Blindness

As a result, the management transferred me to the Gas Laboratory which did not require any titration. I was doing reasonably well there. This was a new subject in the industry and I was being trained by a Belgian technician, Monsieur Jadoh. I became friendly with him. I was the only person working in that section. Fortunately, I got an opportunity of showing the operation of the first Hydrogen-determinator in India to the then Prime Minister Nehru who visited Tata Motors in 1957.

Nehru's Visit to Tata Motors

I remember an episode with Jadoh. One day, both of us were walking on the lawn in front of our laboratory as we had no job at hand. We were waiting for some equipment to come from Belgium. We crossed the Works Manager, Mr. N.G. Chakraborty on the way. He was on his daily visit to the factory. He asked Mr. Jadoh why he was wasting time outside the laboratory. Mr. Jadoh said that he had no work in hand and was waiting for some parts from Belgium expected in a week to complete the task. Mr. Chakraborty advised him to take off for a week and visit Kolkata as he might have go back soon after he had completed his task. Jadoh said that it was a good idea but he wanted to take me along with him as he was new to the country. I said I would not be able to go as I was an apprentice and had no leave due to me. Mr. Chakraborty immediately allowed me a week's paid leave as a special case. This special leave with pay to both of us impressed Jadoh and he commented that Mr. Chakraborty was a great leader. I understood how easy it was to get respect from people by giving small favours. In any case, we had no work at that time and the company did not lose anything. I also remember when the equipment arrived, we worked 12 hours a day voluntarily to complete the task in record time.

Both of us left for Kolkata by train. On reaching Kolkata in the wee hours of the morning, Jadoh checked into the second best 5-star hotel of Kolkata at that time, Great Eastern hotel. On reaching the hotel, I said that I would be going to my uncle's place at Ballygunge and would come to him every day to take him sightseeing. He insisted that I should stay with him at the hotel as he was new to Kolkata otherwise, he would feel uncomfortable. Finally, I agreed. I had never been to a five-star hotel before. I found the hotel was immaculate. Everything was shining.

A double bedroom was assigned to us. There were two large beds. I went to see the bathroom. It was a large one. I found at least 10 different types of spotlessly clean and white towels were there. We started making our beds when a bearer rang the doorbell. He said that we need not make the beds as it was his job. He said that he has been assigned to our room to provide any service and we were not required to do anything ourselves. I suspected that though Mr. Jadoh was a *Sahib* (white person from abroad) to us but back home, he probably had not ever stayed at any five-star hotel either. He refused to take the service of the bearer and we did everything ourselves.

At noon, we went to the hotel bar. Mr. Jadoh asked for a glass of beer. He poured the contents into two tall glasses. He offered one glass to me. I said that I had never had beer before and my family was against it. He said that he had already raised a toast in my name and I had to accept the stuff. Anyway, I closed my eyes and took a sip. I felt that the smell was obnoxious and my throat was burning. I left the glass and said I would have no more. Little did I know that in the future, I would not only take beer but also other alcoholic drinks including whisky.

There were three restaurants in the hotel. One served continental cuisine, one Indian and the other Chinese. We went to the Chinese restaurant for dinner. I had never taken Chinese food before. It was delicious. Next day, we went shopping at the famous New Market. It was a fashionable market for foreigners. I knew that they would ask for very high prices and you could bargain. I advised Mr. Jadoh to bargain and he took my advice. He wanted to buy a silk scarf for his wife. They quoted a price. Mr. Jadoh gave a counter offer of only 10% of the quoted price. Then the bargaining started. Mr. Jadoh went up to 60% of the quoted price. The shop owner gave a counter offer of 80% of the quoted price. The process continued till Mr. Jadoh offered 70% of the asking price. The shopper would not budge. Mr. Jadoh left the shop. Then the shopkeeper requested him to come back and the deal was struck at 70% of the quoted price. I understood how to bargain and arrive at the right price.

There was a shop in the hotel precincts. Its name was Curio Palace. They had fancy items which the foreigners used to buy as souvenirs.

The shopkeeper showed many items but Jadoh would not buy any of these items. They offered him free beer to drink. The next day the same thing happened. I felt a little uneasy that every day he was drinking free beer and was not buying anything. I was surprised that on the third day he bought everything without bargaining. I understood that as a businessman, you must have patience.

Back at Jamshedpur, one day, my boss Dr. U.K. Bhattacharya, slighted me by saying that I could as well be a clerk because I was only a B.Sc. which according to his standard was not a good enough qualification. I started thinking about what I could study further. I did not know the qualification of Dr. U.K. Bhattacharya. I asked some people about his qualifications. They said he was a highly qualified Metallurgist. He was a M.Met from BHU (Banaras Hindu University) and later obtained a D.Sc. from MIT (Massachusetts Institute of Technology), USA. I enquired from people how I could study metallurgy while doing my job. Someone advised me that there was an institution called the Institution of Metallurgists, London. They take examinations from practicing persons working in the metallurgical industry from all over the world. I identified a person at Tata Steel who had passed this examination. I met and talked to him. He discouraged me and advised me not to venture in to this as only two percent of people pass this examination. He said that it was too much of hard work and there was no coaching available.

Whenever I was faced with an adverse situation, I tried hard and succeeded in spite of problems. So, I went ahead and sat for the examination in 1959, just one year after I started studying in Metallurgy. While working in the Gas laboratory, I was asked to also help in the Physical (Mechanical Testing) Laboratory as I had less work load. The head of the physical laboratory was also a simple B.Sc. like me but he had more than 7 years of experience in Mechanical Testing at the Rifle factory, Ishapore near Calcutta before joining Tata Motors. He was a bachelor and used to live alone in his quarter. I used to consult him about my academic studies. He used to try to help but his knowledge was limited.

When I sat for the examination in 1959, I was pretty certain that I would easily pass. But, when the result arrived from the United Kingdom, I found that I had failed miserably in all the subjects. My laboratory friends advised me not to try again as most people fail. All of us were young. The other young men used to enjoy indoor games like carom, billiard, etc. at the company club after duty hours while I used to slog alone trying to decipher subjects like Physical Metallurgy, Foundry Practice, Ceramics, etc. I continued with my efforts even after discouragement from all with even more determination. I became a member of the local libraries including the libraries of National Metallurgical Laboratory, Tata Steel, etc. TELCO did not have any library then. When people found out that I was trying to study seriously, many of them including the librarians helped me. Even the then chief metallurgist of Tata Steel, Dr. Biswanath helped me. Unfortunately, when I wanted to discuss some of the theoretical issues with top metallurgists of Tata Steel, I found that many of them were good executors, but had forgotten the nitty-gritty of the subjects which they had studied a long time ago.

Anyway, after two more years of serious study, I sat for the examination again in 1961. At that time, I was afraid of the result. But when the results arrived, I found that I had passed all the subjects with flying colors. My diploma from the Institution of Metallurgists, L.I.M (Licentiate of the Institution of Metallurgists) was equivalent to Bachelor Degree of Metallurgy (B.Met.) in India. After the results were announced, the company transferred me from the laboratory section and promoted me to the position of Metallurgical Assistant in the metallurgical process section.

I would have been happy to stay at this level with B.Met. equivalent education as I was now considered as a Metallurgical Engineer. But this was not to happen. My practical examination for L.I.M took place at the then famous B.E. College (now known as Indian

Institute of Engineering Science and Technology, Shibpur – IIEST) at Howrah near Kolkata. During the practical examination, the Head of the Metallurgy department, Dr. A.K. Seal commented that L.I.M was not a sufficient qualification. Unless I had a Masters' degree in metallurgy or its equivalent, it would not be of much use. So, I decided to go for the next level of examination known as A.I.M (Associate of the Institution of Metallurgists, London).

If anyone had more than 7 years practical experience in the metallurgical industry, he could sit for the A.I.M Examination directly. My senior at the physical laboratory, Mr. Dipak Roy, had, by that time, more than 10 years of experience. He expressed his desire to study A.I.M along with me and take the examination. To me, this seemed a good opportunity to have someone else to discuss and consult. We used to study together at his flat. He had a good cook who would prepare tea and snacks while we were studying. Now, I could discuss topics with an experienced person who was senior to me in experience.

Although I had spent quite a few years at Tata Motors, everybody at Tata Motors still thought of me as a young trainee as I had been very young in age when I had joined. I was weak in physical stature too. I was not being given due recognition in spite of adding more qualifications. Tata Motors was not prepared to recognize me as a metallurgist but only accommodated me as a Metallurgical Assistant. I felt that I was being ignored. Everybody at Telco used to like and love me but only as a young lad. That was not enough recognition but a consolation. I remember an episode. I was not good at manual jobs. Once while I was working at the Gas laboratory, I broke an important glass vessel. It was a vital part of the instrument without which the hydrogen determination could not be done.

My immediate boss was Mr. Bimal Kumar Gupta. After office hours that day, I went straight to Mr. Gupta's residence and told Mrs. Gupta about my problem. They did not have any children and she used to treat me like her son. She assured me not to worry.

When Mr. Gupta reached home in the late evening, she asked him not to penalize me and find a solution. She said I was too young to do such jobs.

Accidentally Breaking an Important Glass Vessel

I was let off lightly. The glass part was sent to the National Glass and Ceramics laboratory in Kolkata where the critical glass part was repaired. There were many such occasions when I was looked after and cared for. So, it was very difficult for me to make a decision about whether or not to leave Tata Motors and look for greener pastures.

One day, I noticed an advertisement in the newspaper for the post of Metallurgist at New Central Jute Mills (NCJM), Budge Budge near Kolkata. I applied and got the job. Even after I notified my present company, TELCO would not recognize me as a metallurgist. I really wanted to stay. I was in a dilemma. Tata Motors was a renowned company. I had my relatives and friends at Jamshedpur. Now, I would have to leave the comfort of a place where I was being loved and cared for. I talked to one of my top bosses at Tata Motors, Mr. R.J. Bhatwadekar to seek his advice. He was the Head of Central Research Laboratories in Tata Motors. He was also the boss of Dr. U.K. Bhattacharya. He was previously the Head of RDSO (Research Development and Standards Organisation) in Indian Railways. I met him and spoke about my dilemma. He told me that I should leave Tata Motors and find my true self in life. He said that at Tata Motors, people would always treat me as a kid as I had joined as a young apprentice. Mr. Bhatwadekar told me a story about one Mr. Bhattacharya at Indian Railways. Mr. Bhattacharya was a metallurgical graduate from B.E. College (now IIEST) and was a rank holder. He had a beautiful wife and a comfortable job with the Indian railways stationed at Kolkata. Every time, there would be an opportunity for a promotion outside Kolkata, he would decline the job. He was a happy-go-lucky person and enjoyed a good prosperous life with the family. Many years later when the question came to select someone for the position of Chief Engineer at Railways, he was not given the opportunity. By then, his wife was old and all their children were grown up and located outside Kolkata. Now, he was prepared to go anywhere. But the management said that many of his juniors had already surpassed him as he had declined those previous opportunities offered to him. Now, it was too late for him to claim the job. So, Mr. Bhatwadekar asked me to take a leap and take the risk. Most of my friends and relatives, however, advised me not to leave Tatas, as it was a great organisation. Finally, I decided to try my worth outside.

9

Life Outside Tata Motors

In the new workplace in Kolkata, I was still trying to find myself. At Tata Motors, my job was very clear cut. I did not need to make big decisions. Here, I had to make critical decisions of which I was not sure and found myself in turmoil. Of course, I was getting help from my seniors, colleagues and even peers. They used to help me in my work and also advise me on how to take critical decisions. In the meantime, the new company got embroiled in legal complexities like Foreign Exchange Regulations Act (FERA) violation. I used to find police coming to the company every now and then.

I became apprehensive about the stability of my job and applied to another small local company, Howrah City Engineering Company (Pvt.) Ltd. for the position of a metallurgist. They interviewed me and asked me whether I would be able to solve their main metallurgical problems concerning some special types of ferrous metals. If I failed, they would sack me. I took on the challenge and accepted the job. They offered me the job of a Metallurgist and Production Manager. After joining, I found to my utter surprise, that they did not have any order for such products. I took it up with the management. I complained that I did not have any proper job. The management said that they offered me the position in anticipation of getting such orders. They asked me whether I could help them in procuring such orders. I had no sales background but I took this on as a challenge. That was how I became a salesperson.

I would give cold calls to potential buyers and orders started coming in. Over a period of time, I found myself being considered as a good salesman. The company received many high quality orders. And I was also successful in manufacturing those exotic varieties of metal as well.

In spite of such success, I was always afraid of losing my job. So, I would always apply and keep one or two jobs in hand all the time. During one such interview in Bangalore for the position of Metallurgist at the famous government organisation, HMT (Hindustan Machine Tools), I met a chemist from Durgapur Steel. He was very impressed to know that I had passed the metallurgy exam, LIM from the Institution of Metallurgists, London. He was an aspirant for LIM and requested me to join Durgapur Steel as a Metallurgist and arranged for an interview.

I went for the interview. The Chief Metallurgist, Dr. G.P. Chatterjee was a famous person. He liked me and offered a job as Assistant Metallurgist in the grade ₹ 450 to ₹ 1,000 per month. He offered me the lowest in the range at ₹ 450 p.m., whereas I was getting double the salary in my current job as a Metallurgist-cum-Production Manager. Still, I agreed. I thought that this was a stable government job. There would be less pressure on the job and I would be able to focus on my study and pass the next level of examination, A.I.M from the Institution of Metallurgists, London. So, I resigned from my job and gave 30 days' notice.

While I was looking after the production and quality control functions at Howrah City Engineering, a manager named Mr. Biswas used to look after the sales function of the company. Although he was not very qualified, he had worked in sales functions in Germany for a few years. He used to report to the director. I was friendly with him.

After my success in getting orders for special products, perhaps, he felt threatened and did not want me to stay. He might have suspected that the owners might request me to stay back and he might be asked to work under me. I did not realize all this at that time. He invited me to his house one day and told me that the owners might ask me to stay back. If they did so, I should make some tough demands. Perhaps, he thought that the owners would not agree and he would be given full charge of Howrah City Engineering. I asked for his advice. He said that I should demand the following:

1. I should be made Works Manager.
2. I should be given a 20% rise in my salary.
3. I should get a car with driver.

I did not think that they would ask me to stay back and agree to such tough demands. I was packing to go to Durgapur and join the Government job. Twenty-seven days went by and there was no sign of calling me for a discussion. Only three days were left. I was sure that I was leaving. To my utter surprise, on the 27th day, the Director, Mr. M.M. Dutt called me to his office and asked why I was leaving. I said that as a Metallurgist, in my current position, I did not have a high quality job. He said that they had a lot of hope in me and asked what could be done by them for me to stay back. As prompted by Mr. Biswas, I put my terms to him:

1. I should be made Works Manager so that I would have a meaningful job.
2. I should get a 20% raise in salary as I was getting married and
3. I should get a car with driver as I had to come a long way by bus and it was time-consuming.

He told me that he would discuss this proposal with the other board members and get back within two days. The private board comprised of six brothers. I thought it was impossible and was preparing to leave. On the last day, he came back and said that the board had agreed to all my conditions. Now, I unpacked. Immediately after this, Mr. Biswas resigned. I felt sad. Luckily, he started a small analytical laboratory to serve local small-scale industries and became an entrepreneur. I tried to help him with orders whenever I could.

Already, I had taken on the responsibility of sales and quality assurance. Now, I had to take on the entire administration from laboratory to sales to production planning and even personnel management. Of course, finance and purchase remained with the owners. The eldest brother, Mr. J.M. Dutta was the Managing Director. The second brother in the family, Mr. Monomohan Dutta was the Works Director. He was my immediate boss. The youngest brother Mr. N.M. Dutta was the purchase head. Except for one technical person, I had no other helping hand. So, I created a number of files each representing my managers. Whatever, I was doing in each area, I began documenting the actions and results. I was conducting a lot of technical experiments in the workshop as well. I named these experimental activities "Operations Research". Later on, when I studied Management in the UK, I understood that this term, "Operations Research" actually stood for Linear Programming and mathematical problem solving. Anyway, the factory was thriving with orders of many types of products from renowned companies in Kolkata and even outside of Kolkata.

Soon, the news spread that Howrah City Engineering. is a quality foundry and could make sophisticated products, sometimes replacing even imported items. I observed that two senior factory employees, Satya and Ramani were skilled. They were not formally educated but were very good craftsmen. So, I used to look after the metallurgical side and they used to look after all the other technical aspects on the floor. We were getting orders from all over India. It gave me a great feeling of satisfaction. Unfortunately, the owners made no investment in high technology which led to limitations.

I wanted to modernize the factory. There was a very well-known US Engineering Consultancy company at Kolkata known as Kuljian Corporation. I met them and asked them to give us a modernization plan free of charge. I argued that there were hundreds of foundries in the area. If we were successful, they would be able to sell their consultancy work to many of them. They agreed and presented a modernization plan. Now, I asked the management to invest. The works director talked to the other brothers but none were prepared to take the risk. Then, I identified a company named Tested Equipment and Machinery which agreed to invest but only if they were made a partner. I gave this proposal to the owners but they were not prepared to take an outsider as a partner. As it was a family-owned organisation. I felt that there was no scope to improve the status of Howrah City Engineering any further. I started looking for better opportunities elsewhere. I wanted to explore further possibilities for my own growth as a technical person.

In spite of my onerous responsibilities as the Works Manager at Howrah City, I studied alone and sat for the AIM examination and passed. Now, my qualification was equivalent to M. Met. or Master's Degree in Metallurgy. By now, I had started liking academics/ study and found myself proficient in passing examinations. So, I asked the Institution of Metallurgists, London what further examination I could undertake. The institution answered that there were no further qualifications in their institution. The next level was Fellowship which was a honorary status and could only be gained automatically after 10 years of further experience in the metallurgical industry. That was the end of my study of metallurgy.

10

My Marriage

When I shifted to Kolkata from Jamshedpur, my father started pressurizing me to get married. I was 25 years old then and had a reasonable income. My father would seek the help of friends and relatives to identify prospective brides and send me the address. My maternal aunt in Kolkata was the head of the bride search or matchmaking team. She was a beautiful and smart "Kolkata" lady. We had full faith in her choice. We would visit a bride's family, ask her a few questions, eat some sweets and then based on my aunt's opinion and "judgment" decline to proceed further. I used to feel bad about hurting their feelings and had a sense of guilt in "rejecting" them. But that was the practice in those times and everyone accepted the system.

My father would continue to send more leads from different families in and around Kolkata. I remember one such instance vividly. The prospective bride's family used to live in a Kolkata suburb called Uttarpara. The girl had lost her father. Her grandfather was a rich person in Kushtia, Bangladesh. After the partition, they had shifted to Uttarpara. When, we went to see the prospective bride, the grandfather was saying that when Goddess Durga gave wealth, she gave them with ten hands and now she was taking away those riches with one hand. They were becoming poorer by the day. After seeing the girl, my aunt rejected her as she was short and did not have a fair complexion. We got up to leave. The grandfather asked my aunt- what was our decision? My aunt answered that she would discuss with the whole family and let them know the answer. I could see the girl's feet behind the curtains. Perhaps, she was waiting to hear the result with trepidation. I felt very bad for her.

Then my father shared a proposal from Jabalpur. My father-in-law was known to one of my father's friends at Agartala. He brought the proposal. So, one day my father-in-law came from Jabalpur to see me at Kolkata along with his brother-in-law. At that time, I used to stay in a one-bed-roomed flat at an upscale area called Ballygunge. I found out that the brother-in-law, Pulak, had been my school mate at our village in Bangladesh. They were also one of our distant relatives. Both of them decided in favor of me as the bridegroom. I said that my aunt and my brother, Rathindra had to meet the girl and then only a decision would be taken.

They said they would go back to Jabalpur and return with the prospective bride. So, after a couple of months, they requested us to come and meet the girl. They were staying with the elder brother of my father-in law at Kalighat. When we went to their house, we could easily tell that they were an ordinary middle-class family. Upon seeing the girl, my aunt and brother liked her and decided to close the chapter. By the time we left their house, it was afternoon and being quite happy, both my brother and my aunt insisted on watching a movie at the local "Priya Cinema". The movie's name was "Junglee". All three of us thoroughly enjoyed the movie.

Later on, I told my father-in-law that they had to wait for six months as I had to save some money to bring all my close relatives from Agartala and Jamshedpur to Kolkata for the wedding. He asked me how much money I would require for the travel. I told him that it would be around ₹ 3000/-. He said that he would pay the money. I told him that I would need three months to search for a two-bed-roomed house. He agreed. Three months later, I got married at the age of 27.

Our Picture after Marriage

PART-IV

Life after Marriage

75th Birthday Celebration with Family

11

My Family

India is a country that worships women deities and men claim to deeply love their mother, but it is also a nation and culture that values boys over girls and treats women as property and second-class citizens and members in their own families. Somehow, this respect for a statue or representation of womanhood does not get translated into gratitude, appreciation, empathy, let alone respect or worship.

I have two daughters. I am not sure I can be called a "modern" man with "modern values" of equality. Perhaps some biases still persist, which my daughters are constantly trying to enlighten me about. But I have always encouraged my wife and my daughters to be independent and aware of the world. This approach of mine has not been easy for my wife to accept given her protected upbringing in which she was not allowed to study further to complete a master's degree with the concern that the university was co-educational and too far from home. I wanted my wife and daughters to be self-sufficient and prepared for the world and able to manage things even in my potential absence.

Although I don't really think it would have been different if I had sons, I encouraged my daughters to dream, to study at the best universities, shared inspiring stories of great leaders and thinkers. I was not a father who remembered birthdays and anniversaries and sometimes even forgot to pick them up from school. But I spent time with them playing games, writing, sharing poetry and stories, spending days at the parks and lakes in Kolkata. My wife was the disciplinarian in our family.

Strangely even though my father was so strict and demanding of me, I could never bring myself to even raise my voice. Did I evolve to be the father I became because I had vowed not to be like my father was with me, or was it just so much easier to love my dear daughters who were and still remain devoted to me? I don't know.

My way of guiding was to gently suggest, give advice, support their growth and development as adults. Their mother was already doing a good job of control and discipline, for which I am thankful, as I could become the "good cop".

So, when my younger daughter got a full scholarship to study in Wharton, I did not stop her although my heart was crying. When my elder daughter received a marriage proposal and the prospective father-in-law pestered her for two hours trying to extract the response that she would give up her MBA study and would not take a job after her marriage, I controlled my anger and pain. Needless to say, we never spoke of the incident again and we immediately stopped all on-going conversation with the prospective family immediately.

And then again, when my elder daughter too, left the country to pursue her career and we were left alone in the emptiness with two dining chairs staring back at us, I encouraged her to go and soar and fly high, which she did so well.

Today, I am deeply proud of my two daughters who have always stood by my side, who have followed me in my own "experiments with truth", who have carved out a space in the sun for themselves, winning the respect and adulation of so many.

I am also deeply grateful for my two sons-in-law that my daughters chose for themselves. They have supported my daughters and together raised three beautiful and smart grand children who bring a smile to my face and fill my heart with joy.

I ask myself, did I do enough for my wife and my daughters? I honestly wonder if I could have done more. I ask them the same. They tell me I was an "awesome" and inspiring Dad.

Without getting into a debate about women empowerment, I can only express my gratitude for the wonderful women in my life who have brought so much joy, happiness and inner peace. If only more men would realize the joy that can be received when we learn to appreciate how women can heal not just families but the world!

12

Time after Howrah City Engineering

In the meantime, my ability to make different kinds of iron and steel became well-known in the industry and the house of S.K. Birlas' sent someone from Bombay (now known as Mumbai) to take my interview in Kolkata. I was interviewed at the famous Grand Hotel (now known as Oberoi Grand). The position was that of Production Engineer at a place called Thane near Bombay (also known as Mumbai). Although the position was junior compared to the present one I held of Works Manager, I agreed to move as I did not want to waste my life in a small old factory at Kolkata with no scope for growth.

The Birlas selected me provisionally and asked me to visit Mumbai along with my wife and see the place and satisfy ourselves before I joined. They agreed to bear all the related cost of moving. My wife and I went to Bombay. I was very pleased to see the factory set-up. It was a brand-new modern foundry. They had a British Technologist. I was being recruited to replace him. The company, Indian Smelting and Refining gave me a two-bed room flat to stay and provided pick up and drop off by the company bus. I moved to the new company. They gave me the designation of Production Engineer but actually, I had to do the job of a Metallurgist besides looking after production. Here too I could leverage my expertise as a metallurgist.

At Kolkata, I had to make high duty cast iron and malleable iron. Here I had to make S.G. Iron (Spheroidal Graphitic Cast Iron).

This was a new material about which I did not have any prior experience. They had a technical collaboration with a consulting company called, International Mond Nickel. It seems that the British Technologist whom I replaced had not been able to make the product successfully. I requested the company to ask the consultancy firm to show me the production process once. The consultancy firm had a metallurgist called Dr. Sastry. He told me that all the details were already available in the literature provided by them. But I requested them for a practical demonstration at least once. They did so. Thereafter, I read all the books and applied the knowledge given in the literature and we became successful. Soon the knowledge of this success spread in the industry.

Indian Smelting and Refining, near Mumbai

Another company at Nasik near Mumbai, Business Combine Ltd. belonging to the Sahu Jain group started manufacturing this exotic product almost simultaneously as Indian Smelting. They were also not very successful in making this product. They removed their Works Manager, Mr. Mukherjee who promised them that he would be able to make the product but failed.

Business Combine offered me the position of Works Manager with a much higher salary than that of Birlas. They offered me a three bed-roomed bungalow and a chauffeur-driven car. So, I resigned from Birlas. The director of the Birla company, Mr. Singhee called me and asked me why I was leaving. I said that at Kolkata, I was a Works Manager. Here, I was working in a more junior position and required to do even shift duty at times. Moreover, I had recently wedded and my wife often remained alone during nights when I was on night duty. I was also intimidated by the Commercial Manager, Mr. Tibrewalla, who from time to time would call me and scold me for my shortcomings, although he was not my direct boss.

Mr. Singhee said they were happy with my performance. He said that I should not bother about Mr. Tibrewalla. He also said that if someone offered you a soiled hundred rupee note, would you not just say sorry and not accept it. If you do that with Mr. Tibrewalla, you would not suffer mentally. Just ignore the person who abuses you. Mr. Singhee said that they had taken a Works Manager recently and could not replace him just then but he could create a new position of Deputy Works Manager and offer me that. I thanked him and said that once I resigned, I should not re-join. So, that was the end of my career with Indian Smelting and Refining, Thane.

I joined Business Combine Ltd. at Nasik as Works Manager in 1967 and spent the most eventful three years of my life. Indeed, I had a very good time during this period. Nasik was a newly developed town in the state of Maharashtra. It was a formative period for the state. Mr. V.P. Naik was the Chief Minister. He was very dynamic and wanted to industrialize even the remote areas of the state beyond Mumbai and Pune.

At Nasik, there were only two private sector public limited companies at that time. Our company, Business Combine Ltd., was one of the two public limited companies. The other was Bahco Taparia, an Indo-Swiss company. It was a joint venture with an

Nashik Road Railway Station

Indian Promoter, Mr. Taparia. As the Works Manager of a public limited company, I became quite well-known in the small city within a short period. I was made a member of the Junior Chamber of Commerce (JCC) and President of the local Bengali Society.

The Bengali society used to organize many social functions including the famous *Durga Puja.* This was a very popular event among the Bengalis throughout the world. There is hardly any major country in the world where there is no *Durga Puja* event. Wherever there were a few Hindu Bengali families, there would be *Durga Puja* celebrations.

Durga Puja at Nasik almost became an inter-societal event. Many non-Bengalis including the local Marathi population used to participate in the *Durga Puja* celebrations at Nasik. It was not a truly religious event. It was a kind of socio-religious event where Bengali families working at different places got together and enjoyed four days of community food and cultural events. As the President of the Bengali Society, I wanted to popularize it further and make it a big event. Nasik was a place where the army had a big establishment. The army and air force had their own cantonments and bases there. The air force base was at a place called Ozar, in the north-east of Nasik. They also had a working airfield for training purpose. The army base was at a place known as Deolali in the south-west of Nasik. There were many Bengali officers both in the army as well as in the air force. Both the Heads of Army and Air Force were Bengalis at that time. My friends and I from the Bengali Society met and befriended them. They joyfully agreed to participate in the *Durga Puja* celebrations. Apart from the local Bengali society, these Army and Airforce officers and their family members used to take active part in the local *Durga Puja* and this annual event became a gala occasion.

We used to invite renowned singers from Bombay. All of us used to enjoy three/four days of the *Durga Puja* celebrations together enjoying the common lunch irrespective of position or status at the cost of the club. It was a very nice setting where people from all levels of society starting from the bottom level up to the General Manager or the Army Commander would sit cross-legged on the floor and have meals together.

Being a small town, we had nothing to do in the evenings. So, I used to take my young daughter Sutapa and my wife and visit friends and acquaintances in different parts of the city. In Bengali culture, we call it, '*Adda*' where friends and relatives get together and chit chat and discuss various topics ranging from gossip to politics to the sacred texts, sports and more. We used to meet at different person's houses on different days.

The host used to offer tea and snacks, usually vegetable fritters known as '*Pakodas*'. The evenings used to be thoroughly enjoyable.

I had a very nice new bungalow. There were three similar bungalows side by side. These were known as Pingle's bungalows. The owner was a goldsmith named Mr. Pingle. These were some of the best bungalows in the city available at that time. But these were at the outskirts of the city, far away from the centre of the town. Most of my friends were local Bengalis. They used to work in the Government Printing Press and Security Printing press. Their living colony was in the city center. Most of them did not have cars. Often, we would go to their homes in the evenings. When it was my turn to host my friends, they would come by bus. I would drop them back by my car at night because there were no buses plying in the area at late evenings.

One of my close friends was Mr. Baidyanath Bhattacharya. He used to work at the Govt. of India Press. He was very humorous and had a kind heart. Any Bengali coming to Nasik with no address to go to would normally be welcomed at his house. He would host him, for as many days as the person would like to stay. Sometimes, Baidyanath Babu would go to the railway station to see if there was any new Bengali alighting from the train with no place to go to. He would then bring him home. His brother, Bholanath was also kind. Both the brothers were humble and good people and used to help others although they were neither well-to-do nor held high positions in the work place. I had regard for them and liked them. If anyone fell sick or became un-well in the colony, they would take them to the hospital. If anyone came for an interview from out of station for a job at the press, they would take the newcomer to the place of interview and help.

Nasik was a well-known Hindu religious place for pilgrims. If any elderly person came to visit these religious places, they would accompany that person to those places. So, the family was very well-known and liked by almost all the people in the city, from all positions high or low. One of his friends was Major General Ghosh. He was the Commander of the local military hospital. Another friend was Mr. S. Ganguly, the Chief Engineer of the local telephone services. Although both of them held high positions, they became good friends of Baidyanath. Soon, I became their friends too with the help of Baidyanath. There was a private power generation company at Deolali, a small satellite town of Nasik. The General Manager and Head of the company was an elderly Bengali person, Mr. Mitra. Having heard about me from the city folk, he came to see me along with his wife to get acquainted with me. He wanted to meet me and my wife in person. Perhaps, he was curious to know the young man who was the Head of one of the two privately held large companies at Nasik. Having met me, he treated me like his son, perhaps because I was very young. I was only 30 years old then. His own son was a doctor and used to stay at a faraway place in Punjab called Chandigarh. So, I became more or less his "local" son. I and my wife would often visit their house and Mrs. Mitra would treat us like her own children.

At that time, I had a problem. I was suffering from a disease called 'fistula' which was very painful. I had to often go to Kolkata to consult my family doctor. He gave me a lot of medicine, but it did not work permanently. Someone told me that there was a Muslim

Fakir at Nasik. He used to treat people having fistula with some kind of smoke to take care of the pain. Whenever he treated me with smoke, I used to remain fine for a few days. But it would relapse. In the meantime, my daughter Sutapa was suffering from an itching problem. I consulted many renowned allopathic doctors in the city, but nothing was very effective.

One day, Mr. Mitra came to our home and suggested to consult a renowned, local homeopath Dr. Rustomji for my daughter's ailment. I had no faith in homeopathy at that time. Anyway, I agreed to consult the homeopath, though reluctantly. Mr. Mitra looked at me and said since I was going to the homeopath anyway for my daughter's treatment, why don't I consult him for my fistula problem as well. As I said, I had very scant faith in homeopathy. I used to think that these were quack doctors who might have read one or two books on the subject and were treating poor people who could not afford to go to an allopath.

When I went to Rustomji, I found that he had a very big waiting room. I was impressed by the kind of people who came for consultation. Everybody appeared well to do. Some were senior Army and Air Force officers. I also found that the whole room was filled with photographs of saints of different types of faith. There was a beautiful jasmine aroma in the room. I was impressed.

Meeting Dr. Rustomji with My Daughter

When I entered his chamber, I saw a very big white dog quietly lying at his feet. He prescribed the medicine for my daughter. I was reluctant to talk about my problem to him as I wondered how a homeopath could treat my problem when many allopath doctors had failed.

When I got up to leave his room, he asked me whether I was the new manager of the local big company, Business Combine. I answered, 'Yes.' He said, 'I heard from Mr. Mitra that you have a fistula problem. Would you like to give me a chance to treat you?' Reluctantly, I agreed. He gave me one dose of medicine and that was it. Luckily, I found that I became alright after the treatment, forever. I developed great faith in him and homeopathy; thereafter, I used to consult him for all our illnesses in the family.

One day, I asked him about his background. He said that he was a qualified allopath and was practicing medicine in Mumbai. Once he fell seriously ill and was hospitalized at a Mumbai hospital for a long time. On one of those days when he was admitted in the hospital for treatment, he overheard the doctor telling his family members that he would live for only for the next seven days. Then a miracle happened. That night he saw an unknown saintly person come close to his bed and circle the bed seven times. After that, he became fully cured. Neither the doctors nor his family were aware of this incident and everybody was wondering as to how he became cured overnight. It remained a mystery to all.

One day as he was traveling by a local Mumbai train he found that the person next to him had been reading a book and on the cover of the book, there was a picture of his mystery saint. He asked him who was the person on the book cover. The gentleman was surprised at his ignorance. He answered that the picture was of a famous saint called Sai Baba. He was from a small place called *Shirdi* near Nasik. He said Sai baba was no more, but there was a statue of the saint at *Shirdi* where his devotees would pay obeisance.

After that conversation with the traveler, Dr. Rustamji used to visit *Shirdi* every now and then. On one such visit, one night he found a Bengali family crying for help. One of the children in the family had serious diarrhea and the child was almost collapsing. *Shirdi* was a small village, and the nearest hospital was 30 kilometers away. There was no car available in the village. They would have to travel by a cow cart to the nearest town for an allopathic doctor. So, it was a situation where there was no solution and the child could die. Although Dr. Rustamji was a qualified allopath, he used to study Homeopathy books at leisure. He used to keep some homeopathic medicine with him as there was no medical facility at *Shirdi*. He offered the family homeopathic medicine for diarrhea and the family accepted his offer. He gave the medicine and asked for the blessings of Sai Baba. The medicine worked like a wonder and the child recovered. It was at that time that Dr. Rustamji decided to serve the local community at *Shirdi* with homeopathic medicine. He offered his services to the authorities of the Saibaba temple. They agreed to accept his offer. So, he started practicing homeopathy at *Shirdi* as a kind of charity. The homeopath practice had been running well. He left his thriving allopathic practice in Mumbai and started a charitable homeopathy centre at the temple compound.

He was quite happy there and was treating pilgrims on a charitable basis. He used to live on whatever money the patients paid as donation and never asked for money from them. After a while, the temple trust asked him whether he could help them to start a proper hospital. He agreed. But the temple trust asked him to sign some official papers which were false. He declined and left the homeopathy practice at the temple and started his own charitable dispensary in the nearby town, Nasik in the name of Saibaba and named, "Sai Baba Charitable Dispensary". He used to prescribe medicine in the name of Sai Baba and it used to work.

I used to take medicine from him for any ailment even after I left Nasik and went to the UK. I never used any allopathic medicine thereafter for six long years.

It was at Nasik that my second daughter, Sumita was born. She was a baby weighing 10 pounds. She was very beautiful with a head of curly hair.

Unfortunately, the owners of Business Combine sold the company at Nasik after three years of my stay there. So, I started looking for and found a job as the Works Manager at a steel making factory near Mumbai at a place called, Kalwe. During the negotiation period with the new employer, I had to go to Bombay often. Travel from Nasik to Bombay used to take three hours by train. On one of those days when I had an hour's time before I had to board the train, I thought of visiting the British High Commission which was just opposite the railway station.

The Helpful British Angel

I went to the High Commission's library and was reading the Daily Telegraph looking for some opportunity for a job in the UK.

After that one day, it became a practice. Whenever I used to visit Bombay, I would go to the high commission library and read newspapers and hunt for jobs in England. I sent many applications but with no success.

One day, a British lady from the library came out and asked what she could do for me. I said I wanted to migrate to England and sought her advice as to what to do for this. She gave me a set of papers and said I should fill them up and apply. I applied.

After about two months, one day I went to Mumbai to arrange for the modalities of transferring household goods to the new place of work. Like on other days, I went to the library and was sitting at the library quietly and looking at the newspapers. The British lady came again and asked what she could do for me. I said she should arrange for my immigration to the UK. She asked, 'Did you apply?'. I said, 'Yes.' She replied, 'When?' and I said, 'Two months ago'. She said people had been waiting for five years or more. There was no chance of receiving an immigration offer just two months after I applied. I requested her to see whether my name was there, just in case. Reluctantly, she went away and came back smiling and said, 'Yes, you have indeed received an offer to migrate". This was in July 1970.

I informed the new employer that I would not be able to join them and they should look for someone else. That was the end of my job at Kalwe.

While applying for jobs in the UK, I also used to apply for study possibilities there. During that very period, I received an offer to study M.Sc. in Quality Assurance at Uxbridge University, UK. The starting date of the course was 16th September, 1970. I had no passport. I had to hurriedly organize a passport and obtain a visa, if I was to join the M.Sc. course at Uxbridge on time.

At Business Combine, I had a very good relationship with the workmen. Nasik was just getting industrialized. The workmen were new to factory life. There was no union that I could consult with nor had I any labor officer who could guide me. All the nitty-gritty of administration had to be decided by me. I made a list of holidays for the year. I made this based on my own perception.

One day, only two workmen attended the factory. The next day I asked the people why they were absent on the previous day. They were very surprised and said that it was a Ram Navami festival. It was a big religious day for them which I was not aware of. I thought that there should be a forum where I could consult the workmen. We had a bright young factory employee named Sirsat. I sent him to attend a seven-day course on "UNIONISM" at Mumbai. After his return, I asked the workmen to form a union with Sirsat as the Head of the Union. I used to run the factory in consultation with them thereafter.

One day, Sirsat came to me with a proposal. He said that the Ram Navami festival was again approaching. It was a nine-days festival. They wanted a nine-day holiday at a stretch. He said the company had already declared a five-day holiday for *Durga Puja* event. Ram Navami was on the ninth day of that whole festival. Ram Navami lasts for nine days. So, he wanted a holiday for nine days and agreed to work for four days on two consecutive Saturdays and Sundays to compensate. Weekends were normally holidays. So, the company would not lose four days of production, but they would be able to enjoy nine days of celebration at a stretch. I thought it was a fair proposal. The company would not lose any production while the employees could celebrate for the whole of Ram Navami. I gave my consent.

When the local government factory inspector came to know about this, he met me and objected to this decision. He said that I could not do this as per law. According to him, the company must give a two-day break every week and nobody could work continuously at a stretch without a weekly break.

I did not see any logic in his argument as my decision was based on mutual agreement with the workmen. I thought it was fair both to the workmen as well as to the company. In my opinion, the law should be fair to both the parties involved and went ahead. The factory inspector filed a case against me at the local court. This case had been going on for two years.

In India, the legal process is time-consuming. My problem was that I could not get a passport as long as there was a pending legal case against me. I was looking for a solution. I approached the young factory inspector for a solution. He was otherwise friendly with me and suggested that if I approached the court and accepted my guilt, the court would absolve me with some fine. Although I did not morally agree, I approached the court with the proposition and the court absolved me with a small fine. I paid the fine and received my passport almost instantly.

Now, I had to arrange for an air ticket to Heathrow. I went to Mumbai and purchased a one-way ticket to Heathrow via Air India with the travel date as 15th September 1970 so that I could join Uxbridge the next day. Since I had the immigration offer from the U.K. Govt., there was no problem in obtaining a visa. So, all was set for me to go to the UK and attend M.Sc. class at Uxbridge University in time.

In the meantime, I had already packed everything at the house in order to move to my new job in Mumbai. Now, I had to change the program. I was in a hurry.

I decided to send my family to my father-in-law's house at Jabalpur and go alone to England. In those days, it was very difficult to get foreign exchange. I was allowed to take only three British pounds with me. On 14th September, the whole family including my wife, parent-in-laws and children went with me to Mumbai to see me off. Two of my friends including Baidyanath Bhattacharya also accompanied me to Mumbai. I booked three big rooms at Pritam Hotel at Dadar for all of us.

On the day of the journey, I and my two friends went to the airline's office in the afternoon to inquire as to what time I should report to the airport. The person at the desk asked me to show all the papers. I showed all the papers I had with me. He asked me to show the clearance certificate for Yellow Fever. Apparently, a clearance certificate from a doctor was required for Yellow Fever. I had not gone through any travel agent so I was not aware about it.

I began to perspire at the airline office. Nobody could find a solution. Moreover, the clearance certificate had to be a fortnight old. I was advised to go back to Nasik and get a certificate and come after two weeks with a new date of travel. I was in a soup. I had already vacated my bungalow and all my luggage had been dispatched to my father-in-law's address at Jabalpur. All the train tickets for my family to go to Jabalpur were done. On the other hand, I would not be able to join the M.Sc. class on 16th September 1970 as planned.

At 8 pm, there was a change of shift in the Air India office and a new person came to the desk. He asked me about my problem. When I narrated the problem, he asked me whether I could spare 33 rupees. If yes, he could offer me a solution. I said that I was ready for any amount. He told me that there was a person at Chembur who would be able to provide a yellow fever clearance certificate immediately.

We took a cab and went straight to that person. It was 10.30 pm. The gentleman was sleeping. He asked me for which date I needed the certificate. I said that the date should be two weeks earlier than the travel date and the place should be Nasik. He immediately brought out his stamps and we were done. We took the waiting taxi and went back straight to the airlines office and they did the rest of the paper work.

By the time, we came back to the airlines office, it was 12 midnight and the flight was at 2.30 am. We immediately went to the airport via the hotel. At long last, I was on my way to Heathrow. Unfortunately, I had to start my UK journey with a falsehood that did not leave a good feeling for me.

PART–V

Life in UK

13

Days in England

I had a friend named, Biswajit Chakraborty; he used to live at Slough, very close to the Heathrow airport. He came and picked me up from the airport. I stayed at his place. He was a recent immigrant himself and had a rented room with a small kitchen and a washroom. I used to sleep in the same room with him. He had only one single-bed cot. He arranged a low-height bed for me on the floor. I managed somehow. It was a very small room, which was being heated for hardly two hours at night, that too, by a kerosene heater.

After a week, he arranged for me to stay with a Punjabi family, Gupta's at a charge of five pounds per week including bed and food. England being a full employment socialist country, I was allowed eight pounds per week from the social security department. So, I used to give five pounds to the Gupta family and used the remaining three pounds for traveling and other expenses.

Although, I had the position of Works Manager in India, I only managed to secure a job as an inspector at a foundry at Slough. I was neither habituated nor capable of doing heavy manual jobs. I managed to work in that foundry only for a day and came back with torn trousers which I tore while doing an inspection of a heavy Gear Box. That was the end of my factory job at Slough.

Next, I got a job as a Research Associate with the Central Electricity Generating Board (CEGB). Back in India, as Works manager, I was always busy with either technical or sales or labor matters. I used to thrive on chaos. Now, I found myself with a job with very little to do during the entire day. I made a complaint to my boss, Dr. Willowby that I had very little work to do. He said that this was the job of a Researcher. He advised me to study books and journals in the library and to think about new innovative things. So, whenever I had spare time after the laboratory job, I would go to the library and read books and journals. I found it very boring.

I started applying for managerial jobs in any factory. Because of my qualifications and experience, the employers used to call me for interviews but never offered me a job because I had no experience of managing British staff and local employees. This became my handicap. Still, I continued with the process because the potential employers used to reimburse my fares and provide lunch money. I was enjoying visiting various parts of Britain with money provided by potential employers.

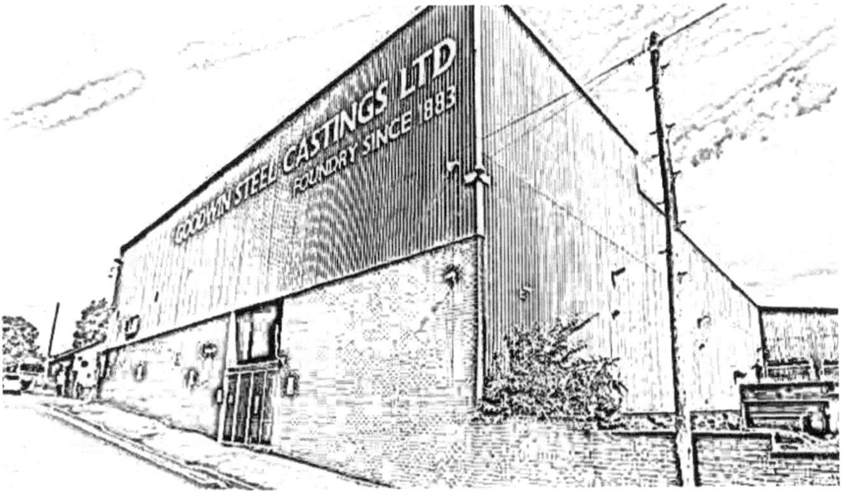

Goodwin Steel Castings Ltd.

On one such occasion, the Chairman of a small company at Stoke-on-Trent called me to appear for an interview. I knew that I would not get the job and the place was far away from Slough where I was staying. I wrote back to him saying that I had no experience in the United Kingdom and that I was an Indian. He answered that he knew that, and I should appear for the interview. I decided to go for the interview, though reluctantly. He sent his own chauffeur-driven Mercedes car to receive me from the railway station. On arriving I was shown the factory by the factory director, Mr. Wheeldon. He took me for lunch at the nearby pub. In the evening, the Chairman, Mr. John Goodwin called me to his office. He was a six-footer with a tremendous personality. He asked for my assessment of the factory. Since I thought that I would not get the job anyway because of my lack of experience in the UK, I thought I would be honest. I told him that there was a criminal wastage of money in his factory. There was scant use of costly equipment. He was dumbfounded because nobody in his company had told him anything like this to his face before, which I was not aware of at that time.

He personally took me to visit the factory again and asked me to show him which equipment was lying idle. I showed him a high-frequency induction furnace which was normally used to make exotic metals. I said if I had this equipment in India, I would have created wonders. Upon going back to the office, he asked me, 'When can you join? I replied that I had to give one month's notice to my present employer, C.E.G.B. He asked me to send the notice to my employer then and there. I said, 'How can I do that without getting any appointment letter? He called his secretary and asked her to type my appointment letter. He asked me, 'What designation and salary do you want?' I answered that back in India, I was Works Manager. I also told him about my present salary at C.E.G.B. as a Research Associate.

On knowing my salary, he doubled it and gave me the designation of Head of the Melting Department to start with and gave me the appointment letter on the spot. I signed my resignation letter from C.E.G.B. and gave it to him to send to my boss. The next day, my research boss called me and said that he was very hurt and felt let down. He said that he liked me and said that I should have, at least, consulted him before resigning from the job. That was the end of my research career.

When I started working at Goodwins, the company organised for me to stay in a hotel for fifteen days. For the first time I had bacon and eggs for breakfast. I found it to be a splendid meal. At work, I started with trepidation as all the workmen were British.

I was the only Indian in the company. But all the managers treated me well. After fifteen days of hotel stay, the company organized a rented flat for me at a place called Longton, very near to the factory. Over time, I seemed to have proved my proficiency and the Chairman felt that I was a good metallurgist and could make any Exotic metal.

One day, my immediate boss, the chief metallurgist, Dr. Billings called me to his office. He told me, 'Robin, I have bad news for you.' I asked him, 'What is it?' He said, 'You are not using good and proper language while speaking to your people.' I replied, 'Could you give me an example?' He said, 'You give them orders directly. You tell them to do this or that."

I said that I always used to speak like this in India. I requested him to advise me what language I should use? He said, "British people do not like to be ordered. You have to tell them politely in an indirect way. For example, if you want somebody to do something, you should say if I were you, I would do it that way". I said I would do so from then on.

One day, I had to arrange the lining of the furnace about which I had complained to the Chairman during my interview. The Chairman asked me to arrange the lining as I wanted. Unfortunately, I was a quality assurance man. I had never worked hands-on in any factory before this. Always, I had acted as a manager. Here, for the first time I was on the factory floor to show the staff how to do a job in practice. So, I called the workmen and gave them a description as to how to do the job as I had learnt from the books.

One of the workers Ted, who was a Polish immigrant, called me to the side and whispered, 'Robin, don't do it this way.' I thought if I did not listen to him, he might jeopardize the work anyway. On the other hand, if I listened to him, maybe it would work and I would get the credit. After all, he was a very experienced worker with shop floor knowledge. So, I said, 'Do it your way but don't let me down.' In India, we used to use Silica-based lining material as we did not have proper basic lining material in India. Here, we had proper basic lining material from Sweden.

I suggested to him to use basic lining material up to the top of the furnace. Ted did not do that. He used basic materials for the entire furnace but gave a shield of acid bricks at the top. The lining lasted 200 heats (200 charges), whereas the average figure previously had been only 50. The Chairman thought I had achieved a miracle. I was then trying to reason with myself as to how Ted's formula worked. I realized that normally there used to be leakage of molten metal from the top of the furnace. As he had given one layer of acidic bricks before basic materials, it must have gelled very hard due to interaction of acidic and basic materials. Actually, people in the factory know more than their managers about the nitty gritty of practical applications. I realized that it was better to rely on the workers.

Over a period of time, I developed a good relationship with all my people. I used to even visit their home at times. One day, I went to visit one of the senior workers, Ken. He used to live in a government-owned free council house. The surroundings of this house were as dilapidated and untidy as an Indian workman's colony. He had eight children, four from his current wife, and four from his previous wife whom he had divorced.

For some time, I was staying at the Longton flat alone. One day, I asked my chairman to help me in bringing my family to England from India. He gave a letter of recommendation and helped me on all the paper work needed to bring my family to England. Nobody in

could be so nice no matter where they came from. Ultimately, someone came with a car from AA and took us home.

As I said that I was not a good driver. In India, I always had a chauffeur. I could only drive but did not know anything of car mechanics. I never changed gear oil neither did I ever top up with water. One day, my car broke down on the way to work and steam was rising out from the engine. Luckily, the car broke down very near to our factory. I left the car on the road and walked to the factory. I explained my plight to my deputy at the laboratory, Steve. He used to call me Robin. He came along with me and exclaimed, 'What have you done, Robin?" There was no water in the radiator!" He arranged for water and the car was back to normal.

Before my family came from India, I was alone at Stoke-on-Trent. Often, Steven would invite me to attend his church on Sundays. I used to go with him. It was a pleasant feeling. Everybody would be given a prayer book and sing hymns in unison. I was doing so along with others. After a few episodes like this, one day he asked me, 'When would you like to get baptized?" I asked where I would need to go for baptism. He said that I had to go a Presbyterian church for baptism as he was a Presbyterian. I thought it over and told him although I liked church and the hymns but I already belonged to a religion. I was born as a Hindu and had no intention of getting converted. He became a little disheartened. He thought he could not save me from Satan in spite of his best efforts. I felt sorry for him.

I realized that sectarian views were not only prevalent in Indian Hindu Society but everywhere in the world. My daughters used to go to a local school and the teachers used to like them. The head of the school liked my elder daughter because she was a quick learner. She had good language skills and used to teach the others in her class. We used to speak to each other in Bengali at home. My younger daughter, Baby could not even ask for a glass of water in English at the school as we spoke only in Bengali. On Parent's Day, the teachers of her school asked me what language we used at home. I said Bengali. They advised me to speak in English at home too and soon, we started that practice.

We were having a good time in England. At the factory, my chairman thought that I was a good metallurgist. He used to bring very difficult orders for me to execute. I remember that at one time, he brought an order from an Indian company, Fouress Business Corporation, Mumbai. They used to make pumps for acid transfer. They wanted a material which was acid-proof. We made it successfully. Thus, I had the good fortune of being considered as an expert in Metallurgy.

During the Christmas festival, we used to get a one week holiday. The holiday used to start from Monday. On the last Friday of the prior week, we used to be at the workplace up to 4 pm without doing any real work.

That meant that all the employees would come to the factory, clock in their attendance and just clean up things and go home by 4 pm with no production done. On the eve of one of these Christmas holidays, my chief foreman, Ken approached me and asked whether I could come to the factory at 3 am on Friday although the factory started at 8 am. I agreed and came to the factory sharp at 3 am. I found that one heat of molten metal (one charge) was ready for pouring into moulds. That meant that the workmen must have had come to the factory by 1 am. It used to take two hours to make one heat ready. Before pouring the metal into the moulds, there was a need to check the composition through a spectrograph. Since the quality assurance person came only at 8 am, Ken had asked me to come at 3 am to check the composition so that they could complete one heat. It meant that the workmen had already completed the production which normally had to be done by 10 am. My team wanted to produce the full day's production by lunch time so that they could enjoy the rest of the time before they left for the Christmas holidays.

I was so overwhelmed by their gesture that I invited the whole team to the nearby pub down the road for a pint of beer. All the workmen had a couple of beers and left for the weeklong holidays. I was lucky to have enjoyed such gestures from my staff throughout my career wherever I worked.

One day, I came across an advertisement on a street wall about a "P.G. Diploma in Management Science", a post graduate program for practicing managers, under the North Staffordshire Polytechnic (now known as Staffordshire University). It was an evening program of three years duration with classes being held from 6 pm to 9 pm. I heard that our chief accountant, Anthony, was going to join the North Staffordshire Polytechnic as a Professor. I asked him for his views about the program. He said that it was a good program and encouraged me to join. And I did.

Since I was working in a factory, my attire used to be comparatively dirty. All the other students, perhaps, worked in offices. They used to attend classes with good attire. Normally, I used to sit at the back of the class to avoid being seen in my soiled and dusty clothes by the rest.

It was very difficult to manage work and also study at night.

I had a small Ford Anglia car. I found it hard driving the car at night. I used to drive at a low speed and I managed. One day, it was drizzling. On the way home after 9 pm, I was driving slowly. The visibility was poor. Unfortunately, I knocked down a local Britisher. He fell down. I stopped the car and suggested that I should take him to a doctor. Luckily, he was not hurt. He said it was not required. I was thankful that the incident did not cause any further problems and the gentleman was unhurt.

During the program, I was required to do a research project. My project was captioned, "Managerial Behavior and Effectiveness". Before I went to England, I had 13 years of work experience in India. I found a lot of difference in the way we managed in India versus how they managed organizations in the UK. That was why I chose this topic.

Knocked Down a British Gentleman on a Rainy Night

My guide was Professor Hubert Kay. He used to teach HR. With his help, I could develop a model of an "Organization". It was based on "Input-Process-Output Model of an organization that was influenced by the External Environment from the outside while simultaneously it was being influenced by the Internal Environment (internal culture) from inside. This model was so dear to me that I used to teach this model to all the students during my whole academic career. I used to call it 'RCB Model No. 1'.

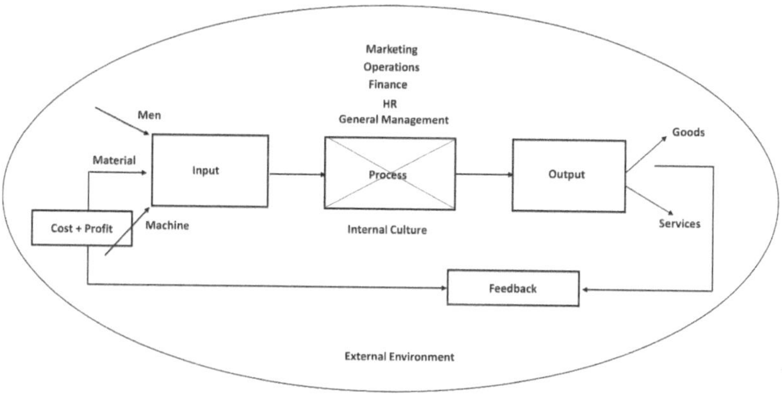

RCB Model No. 1: Organisation as an Input-Output Process

One of my professors at North Staffordshire Polytechnic, Professor, Henry Schermar was a Hungarian immigrant. He used to teach sociology. He had a liking for me. He used to live near my house. Sometimes, I would go to his home. He used to live alone. At other times, he used to visit our house. During the communist rule in Hungary, he had to leave his country due to his views in favor of democracy. He took asylum in England. I remember him fondly.

One day, my course ended. I felt a sigh of relief that at long last, I would not be required to miss my evenings any more. But my life had other twists and turns. One day our principal, Prof. Roy Brace called me to his office. He said I should study MBA. I asked him, 'Why?' He said that I had secured the highest in the class of 1974. They would like me to go for further studies. I said that I was a family man and could not manage the funds. He said they would help me in raising a bank loan of 1,000 pounds and this should be enough to see me through. I said that a two-year course was too long for me. I would have to stay in a hostel. How would my family stay on their own for two long years? There were three business schools of repute then. London Business School and Manchester Business School courses were of two years duration. But, the duration of the third Business school, Cranfield Business School was only one year.

Cranfield Business Course was only applicable for those students who had more than five years' managerial experience. Hence, he said that I would qualify.

Prof. Brace said that I would have to appear for an entrance examination. I applied for the entrance examination. The questions were very different than those I was used to. These were like GMAT which I was neither aware of nor trained for. I sat for the examination without any coaching. Luckily, I passed the examination. Then I was asked to appear for a group discussion and finally a personal interview. At the group discussion, I observed that all the applicants were smarter than me and were mainly of British origin. I was the only brown person from India in that group discussion. Somehow, I successfully completed the whole process.

Ultimately, I received a letter of invitation to join the program. I went to the Chairman of my company, Mr. John Goodwin. He was furious. He said I did not need an MBA and I was a good enough as a Technologist. He offered me a 20% increase in salary and asked me to consult my wife before I took a decision. I spoke to my wife about this offer. My wife was very happy that I would be earning 20% more.

I reconciled myself for that evening. But I had a restless night. At the end of the night, I asked myself, 'Why should I not study"? I had never studied for a proper full time management program although I had been a manager for a long time. The next day, I met the Chairman and said, 'Mr. John, I wish to leave.' He told me that I was doing a wrong thing. He offered me a big new car and asked me to consult my wife again. I had a small second-hand car. Now, I would own a brand new car of my liking. My wife was thrilled. She was very happy. In the evening we went to a nearby car showroom to look at a new Audi. I started imagining myself driving a new Audi car from the very next day. I felt very happy. I slept well that night. Again, at the end of the night, I thought to myself, "why should I not study just for a new car"? Maybe I would drive even bigger cars in the future. Again, the next day, I told my chairman of my decision to leave.

He said if I was so determined to study MBA, he would arrange for me to study MBA in the evenings in the nearby city of Wolverhampton. His offer of extra salary and the new car would still remain. As usual, my wife was very happy with the new proposal. She said that Mr. Goodwin was very right. In this way, I would earn more money, own a big new car, and also receive my MBA. Again, at night I felt the same way as before. I decided to go for a full-time course.

Mr. John said that he would need time for finding my replacement and suggested that I write to Cranfield Business School to retain my seat for one year and he would get my replacement within that year. I wrote and Cranfield agreed. I reflected again and decided not to lose even one year. I stayed on for 30 more days as per my terms although I did not give any formal letter of resignation. At the end of 30 days when I left the job, Mr. John neither paid me the salary for the last month nor gave me any certificate.

That was the end of my job at Goodwins.

14

Days in Cranfield

When I joined Cranfield, I had to stay at the hostel. I would travel to Cranfield every Monday in the early morning and return home every Friday evening. Cranfield was at Bedford near London. It was 120 kilometers away from Stoke-on-Trent. Luckily, during that period, my wife got a job in a famous porcelain factory for a year. My daughters would walk to school alone. My wife used to keep the house key underneath the door mat. My daughters would come back from school by 4 pm and my elder daughter, Sutapa would use the key and open the door. By 6 pm my wife would return from work. As I look back on this, it seems to me that it was an almost inhuman decision.

It must have been a very hard time for all of them. I used to call my wife every night using a two pence coin from the pay phone for each call. I would only say two things: ask how they were doing and tell them that I was okay.

Those were the only things I could manage to say before I had to put more money into the pay phone. I used to come back every weekend and do the grocery shopping for the whole week and return to Cranfield again each Monday morning.

One of my classmates used to stay nearby. He offered to pick me up every Monday and drop me off on Friday, provided I paid the money for the petrol. I thought it was a good idea as I was finding it difficult to travel such long distances with my old Ford Anglia car. In the later part of the course, however, one outgoing Arab student from Cranfield wanted to sell his almost new Japanese Datsun.

Cranfield School of Management

He offered it to me at a throw-away price as he was going back home. So, I bought his car and sold my old car.

Almost 25% of the students in my class were from Oxford and Cambridge. They were very brilliant. During group discussions, I used to admire them because of their creative thinking. However, I was very popular in the class and all the professors knew me because I used to be mostly one of the first in asking questions. You can always think of one or two things. During the latter part of the discussion, complex ideas used to arise, and I used to write down the contents of these discussions. I used to admire my brilliant classmates. I used to reflect on these complex contents and used them in my exam answers. I had to leave the UK before convocation because I joined BOC in India. So, I did not receive my graduation certificate in hand.

I requested the Finance Professor, Dr. D.R. Middleton to give me a certificate. He wrote that I was in the first quartile of the class. I thought that it was a creditable achievement for me given that 25% of the class came from Oxford and Cambridge and many good students came from all over the world. In fact, I never studied in an English medium school. There were only four of us from India. I joined the course from the UK and managed my expenses by taking a loan from a UK bank. The other three Indians came from wealthy families and came directly from India to study with their own money.

I joined Cranfield School of Management, leaving my job at Goodwins. So, after the completion of the course, I had to search for a job. A gentleman named Dr. Sharan came from India for campus interview at Cranfield. He was looking for a fresh MBA from the UK as a trainee for Indian Oxygen Ltd (IOL).

He took my interview but did not offer the job. Perhaps, he thought I was over-qualified for a management trainee job.

In the meantime, I got an interview from a famous consultancy house, Davy Ashmore at Stockton-on-Tees. They gave me a job as a Business Analyst. But I was not keen on a consultancy job. I appeared for a few more interviews and finally got a job in Brazil as a Manager. At that time, Brazil was in the process of industrialization. One of my acquaintances from Stoke-on-Trent had just moved over to Brazil. I was determined to go to Brazil to explore further opportunities. I began working on the moving process.

While I was making the preparations including the visa to go to Brazil, something happened. One day my wife came rushing to me with a copy of the Daily Telegraph newspaper to show me that there was a job advertisement for the position of General Manager in Indian Oxygen Ltd. (IOL). It was a wholly-owned subsidiary of British Oxygen Ltd. (BOC), UK. I told her that I had already been interviewed by their Training Manager at the campus and he had not chosen me even as a Management Trainee. So, there was no question of them hiring me as General Manager.

She insisted that I should at least try.

I said, neither did I know anything about the gas industry, nor did I know anything about the company. So, why would they hire me as their General Manager. I was very skeptical. My wife was the only child of her parents and wanted to go back to India. Finally, I thought about it and felt that I should, at least, give it a try. Brazil was too far away from India. If we could go back home, she would be able to meet her parents after six years. Ultimately, I agreed to try for the General Manager's job at BOC-India.

The initial selector was the Head of BOC-International at their Head Quarters at Hammersmith House in London. I made an application and the head of BOC(I)-HR, Mr. Peter invited me for an interview. He insisted that I should bring my wife with me to London. He wished to speak to both of us at Hilton Hotel over tea.

Since my friend, Bishu Chakraborty was living at Slough, near London, I drove to his house along with my whole family on the day prior to the interview.

I and my wife went for the interview the next morning. At the end of the interview, Peter said that while he had selected me provisionally, I would have to be interviewed by the Chairman and MD of Indian Oxygen Ltd., Mr. Keith Hartley before the final selection.

Later on, I came to know that Mr. Peter was the Global HR Head whose main job was to select talent for top positions for all the forty-nine group companies all over the world. Mr. Hartley was supposed to come to London within the following three weeks. Although I was being chased by my new employer in Brazil to join quickly, I decided to wait for the outcome from BOC-International.

Mr. Hartley came after three weeks. I had a good meeting with him. He was short in height and was a cheerful person with a happy demeanor. He asked me to give him three reasons why I should join IOL. I said that first, it was a sound company where people could work for a lifetime and retire at the end of their career. My father-in-law's elder brother retired from IOL company as a design engineer after forty years of service. The second reason was, the company was prepared to take risks. They were taking an outsider from the industry like me as General Manager who did not have any experience in the gas industry. The third reason was, being an Indian I would like to work and settle down in India.

He asked me my age and how long I had been in the UK. I told him my age was around 40 of which I had been in the UK for about six years. He calculated and said that I was not an Indian but he was an Indian. He said that he had served in the British Army during the second world war in India and joined IOL after the war and stayed on even after the country gained independence. He joined IOL as the Branch Manager at Asansol and his Indian experience was more than 40 years. Both of us smiled and I had to admit that he was more of an Indian than I.

He said that he liked me but I had to be interviewed by my immediate boss, Mr. S.D. Singh before I was on board. Mr. Singh came after two weeks. He was a Punjabi with a turban and beard.

During the discussion, he mentioned that I had no experience in the industry and all the senior people working under me were qualified engineers with more than 25/30 years in the field.

He wondered as to how would I manage my people? I asked for his advice. He said that he would recommend that I undergo two months training in BOC UK, before I moved over to India. I agreed to his proposal provided I was paid salary for those two months. He agreed but said that it would be paid in Indian Rupees after I joined IOL.

The selection process was over. Now, I was waiting for an appointment letter from Indian Oxygen Ltd. More than one month elapsed after the last interview but there was no sign of any such letter. I told my wife to pack and be ready for the move to Brazil. She suggested I give a call to Peter before I took my final decision. I did. Peter said that he was equally astonished why there was no letter even after a month.

He said that he would immediately inquire from the Indian company and get back to me. Soon, he rang me to say that the Chairman of IOL, Mr. Keith Hartley had died of a sudden heart attack. There was now a vacuum at the top. The company management was yet to decide as to who should sign my appointment letter in the absence of the Chairman.

There were two Indian contenders for Chairman and MD's position and there was no decision as to who should sign my appointment letter. Hence, there was some delay in issuing my appointment letter. Finally, BOC International decided to send another British person from London as Chairman and MD in due course. In the meantime, both of the incumbents were made Deputy Managing Directors (DMD) and BOC asked them to manage the functions between them in the interim.

One of them, Dr. S. Chakraborty was the Company Secretary. He was asked to head the HR function as well. The other DMD, Mr. P.C. Basu was made the Head of the Finance and Marketing functions. Finally, Dr. Chakraborty signed my appointment letter. Two weeks later, I received the appointment letter signed by Dr. Chakraborty and finally, my move to go to Brazil came to a halt.

Before going for the training at BOC-UK, I went to the Stoke-on-Trent public library to search for any literature on Industrial Gases. I identified a book called, "Out of Thin Air" relating BOC-UK's fight with Air Products, USA. This was a saga of Air Products, USA's entry into the UK industrial gas market, and defensive commercial and legal fight by British Oxygen UK to retain its market share. It had been dominating the UK Industrial Gas market for many years. This book gave me a considerable historical background knowledge of products, processes, and technological position of the major companies in the industry. I gained a good idea of their strengths and weaknesses. Hence, when I went back to India, I found that I had enough knowledge about the industry which others were not aware of. Since then, I have been known in the Indian Gases industry as an expert. Even today, the All India Industrial Gas Manufacturers Association (AIIGMA) has retained me as the honorary technical consultant with a request to attend all their yearly techno-commercial seminars in India and abroad and judge the technical papers at the seminars.

As per the advice of the Director-Gases Division, Mr. S.D. Singh, BOC-International asked me to spend two months in visiting their various plants and other business units in the UK. These two months were very fruitful. I spent one week at the International Head Quarters at Hammersmith, London. It was a magnificent building just opposite Hammersmith metro station in the heart of London.

One day during my training period, I was spending time with Dr. Wingfield. He used to look after all the sister companies of BOC-International for the entire South East Asia. BOC-International was divided into a few regions like Europe, North America, Africa,

India and South East Asia, Australia, etc. BOC had subsidiaries in all the countries under the British Empire.

I was learning things about BOC's operations in South East Asia and had a sumptuous lunch with him at the company cafeteria. Suddenly at 4 pm., he said "Let us go for a pint of beer". I was surprised. Beer during office time, I exclaimed. He said that one of the employees was retiring after 40 years of service and there was a farewell function at 4 pm. This confirmed my belief that BOC was indeed a company where one could work till the end of his career.

At BOC-International Head Quarters, I met another person called Mr. Rice. He was the International Planning Manager. He told me a very important point. He said that if oxygen was the gas of today, nitrogen would be the gas of tomorrow. While hydrogen would be the gas of day after tomorrow. He said that air contains 75% nitrogen. It is the major product available in air. But BOC had concentrated on oxygen and overlooked nitrogen as a product for a long time. Air Products, USA saw that potential and grew in the nitrogen field. Nitrogen had been finding new uses in pharmaceuticals, chemicals, petrochemicals and other new generation industries. At that time, BOC had a 75% market share in oxygen and only 25% in nitrogen in the UK. The new competitor, Air Products put emphasis on nitrogen and had 75% market share in nitrogen and only 25% in oxygen. That was a good entry strategy for the new comer without having a direct competition with BOC.

He said, slowly fossil fuel availability would reduce and the world would have to look for an alternative source of fuel and that could be hydrogen. He explained that the source of oxygen and nitrogen was free air. Similarly, one day, hydrogen would be generated from free water. The use of hydrogen as a fuel source was yet to happen. This still remained as a potential for the growth of the industrial gas industry in the future.

He also said that the demand for high purity and other exotic gases would grow in future. All this information helped me in thinking strategically about the industry. When I joined IOL, I gave priority to Nitrogen and also to High Purity Gases with good results.

After spending some time at International Headquarters, I was sent to the divisional headquarters of UK West. Their office was in Birmingham and the building was known as Westox House. I visited their tonnage plants and learned about the products and processes. Then, I was sent to the largest compressing station in the UK where they used to convert huge quantity of liquid gases into cylinderized gases for sales to retail customers and dealers. There, I met Mr. David Parr who was the branch manager then. I learned a lot from him. He said I should write down whatever I was hearing. Then I should make a synopsis and utilize that knowledge in India. It proved to be very good advice.

After a couple of weeks, I told the people at BOC-International that they were showing me plants of 500–1000 tons/day size whereas Indian Oxygen's biggest plant size was 12.5 tons/day.

They said that all the plants in the UK were from 500 ton to 1000 tons per day. If I were to see a plant of 12.5 tons/day plant in working condition, I would have to go to Northern Ireland. That made sense but I refused to go. In those days, Northern Ireland was torn by civil war between Protestants and Catholics.

There was a Catholic terrorist group known as the IRA demanding separation of Northern Ireland from the UK and the two sects Protestants and Catholics used to kill each other almost every day. I was worried.

As a compromise, I was advised to visit southern Ireland instead which had a 50 tons per day plant. I visited southern Ireland and saw their operations. It was a one-site operation in a small country. I was happy to see some manual activities at long last. In the UK, they were dealing with large liquid tankers. Therefore, there were only a few people engaged, with limited manual operations.

The Managing Director, Mr. Tom Jago was the sole boss and used to manage everything from his office. He was proud of their medical sales and asked me the sales of IOL medical gases. My only knowledge of IOL at that time was from a balance sheet of IOL which I had obtained from BOC-International. I looked at the balance sheet and told him the figure. He boasted their medical sales was three times that of IOL.

I said that Ireland was perhaps one-tenth the size of India and much less in terms of population. Ireland, at that time was one of the least developed countries in Western Europe.

I said that if India could become a little better economically, India would have the business potential of many times that of the Irish medical business. So, when I came to IOL, I laid special thrust on medical gases and it grew tremendously.

IOL paid for our business class air tickets to India by British Airways. I told IOL authorities that I would like to land in Bombay first and visit Nasik before going to Calcutta. They agreed. While in the UK, I had a swelling in my right hand.

My doctor, Dr. Sanyal said that it was a disease called ganglion and it would never go. It could be operated but it might resurface somewhere else in the body. I thought it would be odd for people to see a swollen hand when I needed to sign papers. I had great faith in my homeopathic doctor at Nasik, Dr. Rustomji. I went to him straight from Bombay. He gave some medicine and said not to worry and that the swelling would go away. After landing at Bombay, we went to Nasik and from there we went to visit Shirdi Saibaba Temple for His blessings before I joined IOL at Calcutta.

When I came to Calcutta, my parents-in-laws came from Jabalpore to receive us at the airport. My father-in-law had no faith in homeopathy. He thought my hand would remain swollen forever. Days were passing by in Kolkata but there was no sign of the swelling going away. It was almost two weeks and the hand condition was the same as before. I also started having some doubts. After about fifteen days, I woke one morning to find that I had no swelling. It had gone forever.

PART-VI

Back Home in India

R . C . BHATTACHARYA
22nd Advanced Management Program (7 - 27 june 1981)

15

Journey at IOL (BOC-India)

While explaining the IOL culture I would like to say that it was like a family.

When I came back to India, the head of HR at IOL, Mr. Anil Sengupta met me at the Bombay airport which I had not expected. A few days later, when I landed at Kolkata airport, he sent one of his assistants, Mr. Arun Dasgupta to receive me at the Calcutta airport. I was housed at the guest house at 4 Mayurbhanj Road which was on the first floor of my Director's Bungalow. We reached the guest house in the afternoon. Although the guest house had a cook, Mr. Arun Dasgupta brought some home-cooked fish for us. I thought the company culture was a homely one. They welcomed and made a new comer like me feel as if I was one of their own.

I joined as the General Manager-Operations of the Gases Division. There were three divisions. Gases division was the largest in manpower and revenue. The second one was the Welding division while the third division was the smallest, known as Plant and Engineering division. The day after joining the office at Kolkata, the General Manager of the Plant Division, Mr. S. Chakraborty invited me for lunch at the Calcutta Club. After about a week, the Deputy Managing Director, Dr. S.K. Chakraborty invited me and my wife for lunch on a Sunday. My impression deepened that IOL was like a family.

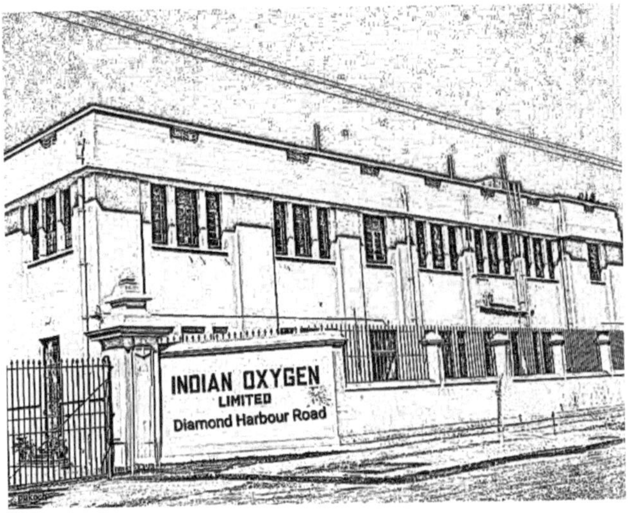

Picture of IOL Regional Head Quarters, Kolkata

My Initial Years at IOL

I joined the company in early 1976. I was given the portfolios of production, marketing, and technology, although I did not know anything of these functions as related to the gases industry. All the people working under me were qualified engineers from JU (Jadavpur University), CU (Calcutta University), IIT (Indian Institute of Technology) etc. and even some with foreign qualifications having more than 25 to 30 years of experience in the field. I used to call them in groups for meetings and would ask their opinion about any problem at hand. I used to listen to all of them intently and used to give my decision based on the majority view and my own instinct.

Almost always, it used to work, and soon I became known as a competent gas professional in the industry. During my stay at Indian Oxygen Ltd. (IOL), I had the opportunity of visiting many sister companies belonging to British Oxygen International like Bangladesh Oxygen (BOL), Malaysian Oxygen (MOX), Singapore Oxygen (SOXAL), Thai Oxygen Ltd., Lien Hua (Taiwan), a joint venture company with a local promoter, BOC-Australia, BOC-UK, and many other places.

The visits were interesting and educative. I adopted many good ideas from the operations of those companies. One idea of importance which I adopted was that of "Application Development". Products like oxygen, nitrogen, argon, etc. were generic products. These products would remain the same but one could always find newer applications of these products in different industries for different uses. For example, oxygen could be used for metal cutting in the fabrication industry but it could also be used to increase productivity in steel melting or as medical gas for respiration in a hospital. I laid stress on this activity and the total market in India started expanding. As a result, price competition reduced tremendously. IOL was the most dominant company with about 70% market share while almost all others were either medium or very small in size without any technological capability. IOL remained as the main technical path finder while others followed IOL's footprint.

Of course, my knowledge from the initial training at BOC-UK was very helpful. I used all my knowledge gained to motivate the team for business growth. My Marketing team was a young lot who had graduated in Business Management from IIM-Kolkata, XLRI etc. They were charged up and took up the challenge.

My Experience in Industrial Branding at IOL

I knew very little about the company or gas industry. Yet, as the General Manager-Operations, I had the task of leading three functional groups, namely, Operations, Marketing, and Technology. My predecessor was a British expatriate from the UK, Mr. Mike Lyal. I never met him. He had divided all the products of the Gases Division into four groups, namely, ASU (Air Separation Unit Gases), F&MG (Fuel and Medical Gases), Industrial Services (mainly medical pipelines) also known as Installation Engineering and Speciality Gases.

Each product group had three persons, one with the knowledge of production, one with the knowledge of marketing, and the third was a finance person. Their role was to design the production and marketing policy for each product group. I felt that it was a good idea.

When I was under training in BOC, UK, one day I had a session with the Head of Planning, Mr. Rice. He told me that Speciality Gases was a new product group and had been growing at 50% in sales value per annum in the UK. In India, it was still taking shape. One of the engineers named Mr. A.B. Giri was dealing with Speciality Gases. He was a young engineer from Jabalpur with an MBA from XLRI, Jamshedpur. He was very enthusiastic. During the budget session, a question arose as to what should be the revenue target for Speciality Gases. Out of thin air, I named a figure. I said it should be ₹ 100 lakhs. Since it was a very new area, nobody knew how the future would turn out to be. Somehow, with the help of Mr. Giri at the factory end and with the effort of the sales people in the field, we reached a revenue of Rupees 100 lakhs that year.

Next year, at budget time, the same question arose as to what should be the new target. I suggested Rupees 150 lakhs and we achieved that. So, like in the United Kingdom, we were also growing at a rate of 50% in sales value per annum. This became a hot subject and the competitors started claiming that they were also offering the same products although I knew they did not have the capability of producing these exotic products.

That was the time I thought of branding these products to differentiate our products from those of the competitors. So, I put up four billboards at the four airports in India, namely in Kolkata, Bombay, Delhi, and Chennai, saying that we had Special Gases in our offering.

The competitors followed us. They also bought billboards next to ours saying that they had Special Gases in their offering. Now, I had a predicament. How could we say that our products were genuine and different? I realized that most of these gases were pure gases. So, next time, I advertised on the billboards that our products were PURE gases instead of calling them just special gases. Again, the competitors copied our strategy. They also said that they were offering PURE gases. I was in a real dilemma as to how to differentiate our products. I consulted our company lawyers and raised a question about how to stop the competitors from using our coined names. Their advice was that anybody could use the words SPECIAL or PURE. Because they were generic words. We would need to use unique names and legalise them as our trademarks.

We gave the task to a renowned communication consulting company, named Clarion. The CEO of Clarion, Mr. S. Sengupta was a specialist in the Branding of FMCG products but he had no experience in branding of industrial products. He started conducting workshops with our marketing staff, many of whom were IIM/XLRI graduates. But they could not identify any unique name for these products even after six months.

After discussing with Mr. Giri and other technical people, I understood that in terms of purity, our products fell into three groups. The highest purity was 10 VPM (10 volumes per million impurities). These were used in research work. The next variety was 50 VPM (50 volumes impurity per million) and was mostly used for analytical purposes. The last variety had the lowest purity. It was 150 VPM (150 volumes per million impurities). These were used in high volumes in factories as process gas to produce high technology products like stainless steel.

So, I created the names 'Research Gases', 'Analytical Gases' and 'Technical Gases' for these three varieties. When I went to the lawyer, he said, these words could also be used by our competitors as well because Research, Analytical and Technical words were generic words. Anybody would have the liberty of using those words. I was at a loss.

One evening, I was sitting on the balcony of my flat at 28/2, Rashbehari Avenue, Ballygunge with a cup of tea. I had been completely absorbed in thinking about the name. Suddenly, I came up with an idea that I could possibly name these three varieties as, 'IOLAR' (IOL Gas for Advanced Research), 'IOLAN' (IOL Gas for Analytical Purpose), and 'IOLAT' (IOL Gas for Advanced Technology). I consulted our lawyers, Khaitan and Company. This time they said that these names were perfectly ok. Nobody could copy these words as IOL was our company brand name because of usage for over 50 years in India by then. Next morning, I went to the Chairman, Mr. K.D. Moore for his approval. He said, 'Robin, why do you want to have three different names? Let us make it, IOLAR 1, IOLAR 2 and IOLAR 3.

I consulted the lawyers again. They said that this was very much acceptable. Although I was a bit unhappy that my original names were not approved, I went ahead because without the Chairman's approval, I could not proceed.

The Head of Production of these products, Mr. Giri, raised a question. Since these were essentially the same products, how would he differentiate the products while delivering different brands to different users? He said that it would cause misunderstanding with customers and sales people. I was now confronted with another problem.

He said that almost all of these were pure products coming from the same purification process. I said it was very easy to solve this issue. We knew that most of these products were good and were of the best variety. For differentiation, we could check individual cylinders for every type of impurity and give a certificate to that effect for every cylinder. These products would be termed 'Iolar 1' which had the most rigorous quality check. Next, we would take one sample out of a batch of 50 cylinders and check the purity. We would offer a batch certificate for those products. Such batch-tested products would be termed 'IOLAR 2' .

We would not mention individual items of impurity and give a batch certificate. Left over balance of the products would be sold as 'IOLAR 3' as we were sure that none of these products would have an impurity level of more than 150 VPM. This process was acceptable to my production and quality control staff as sufficient differentiation in the quality control process and the problem was resolved.

The next question was how to price these products. I found that these products were being purchased from the United States at a price of Rs. 110 per cubic meter and it used to take six months to get the product after a lot of paper work and approval from the government. I suggested that we offer a price of Rupees 100 per cubic meter for 'IOLAR 1'. This would allow all the researchers to use our products without going through a lot of license formalities and yet save 10% of the money. I priced 'IOLAR 2' at Rupees 75 per cubic meter. I reasoned to myself that this was fair because I did not have to involve a lot of costs for individual cylinder testing and the volume purchased was more. The third variety, 'IOLAR 3', was priced at Rupees 50 per cubic meter. Since I knew that the cost of IOLAR 3 gases would be a miniscule of the total production cost.

This low price would allow customers to use these exotic gases in bulk in manufacturing processes. I was not sure whether this was the first industrial branding in India or not but it was a great success. For many years into the future, people would talk about 'IOLAR 1', 'IOLAR 2' and 'IOLAR 3' in generic terms, and our products became synonymous with the industry standard. That was of great satisfaction for me.

Friction with Other Divisions

As I said that IOL had three divisions. The Gases Division used to produce and sell their products and it was the largest division. The second division was the Welding Division. They used to only produce and the selling was done by the Gases Division as the same sales force could do both the jobs since the customers were mostly the same. But there used to be friction between these two divisions.

The sales people in the gases division were mostly science graduates while the production people in the welding division were mostly engineering graduates. The Gases Division people would complain about the quality of the products being sold and the Welding Division used to blame the Gases Division people as not being fit to sell technical products.

The third division was producing and selling industrial gas plants and equipment and was a standalone division. They were helping the smaller competitors of the gases division and thereby also increasing competition in the merchant market. Hence, in a way, the third division was creating and strengthening our competitors. Whenever a potential small-scale industrialist would come to me to inquire about the demand-supply gap, I would discourage the potential investor and advise him not to put up a small plant as it would not be cost-effective. When the same person would go to the Plant Division, they would encourage the same person to put up the plant as he would be their customer. They would suggest to the same industrialist that they should build their plant in a remote place that did not have any production base presently and that would have low overhead compared to IOL.

Actually, these small-scale industrialists were owner-managers with very little overhead and used to compete comfortably with us from locations in distant areas at lower prices as industrial gas could be effectively sold by IOL to customers up to a maximum distance of only 100 kilometers due to high transportation costs.

Regionalization of Gases Division and My Transfer to Bombay

We had 12 gas manufacturing factories in different locations in the country. Every evening, my director used to call all the 12 factory managers one by one and discuss with them if they had any problems. I had to be present at that time to give my opinion or advice. Generally, the meetings used to start at 6 pm and end at 9 pm. I was missing my evenings with my family and friends.

IOL had the culture of inviting an important personality every year as a consultant to interact with the managers. This was a good learning opportunity. For example, one year, IOL invited the head of Strategy, Mr. Khanna from the famous cigarette company, ITC. That year we learned about SWOT (Strengths, Weaknesses, Opportunities and Threats) analysis although I was already aware of SWOT analysis from Cranfield. It was an important concept in Business Schools in those days. Another year, we had Prof. Dr. M.B. Athreya, a PhD from Harvard. He talked about Ethics in Management.

Yet another year, IOL brought a Professor, Dr. K.K. Bhattacharya from Harvard. During my studies either at Staffordshire or at Cranfield, I had never heard of Michael Porter. I was the Head of Marketing of the Gases Division at that time. Dr. Bhattacharya asked me whether I had read Michael Porter. I answered in the negative. He said that in that case, I knew nothing about Marketing. Thereafter, I bought the first book of Porter on "Competitive Strategy" and thoroughly enjoyed it.

Dr. Bhattacharya was a specialist in Management Structure. He talked about this concept. After listening to Dr. K.K. Bhattacharya, I asked my boss, Mr. S.D. Singh whether we should reorganize and restructure the Gases Division. Instead of 12 units, we could divide the units into four regions of three factories each. The head office then would have to interact with only four regional heads and they, in turn, could manage the units under them. In that case, we would not be required to deal with all the 12 managers at the same time. The regional heads would also gain experience for the next promotion or role.

Simultaneously, the unit heads would have a chance to grow in experience and status over time and could potentially become regional managers. He agreed to my suggestion and asked me to prepare a proposal. I divided all the factories geographically into 4 regions—Eastern, Western, Northern and Southern. The divisions were based on each region's revenue and geographical contiguity. After some discussion, the western region was merged with the Northern region and finally, there were only three regions—Eastern, Southern and North-Western. This was because the northern region including Delhi and Kanpur units were too small in revenue. Northern India was comparatively less developed then. West was the biggest market with the highest growth rate at that time. After restructuring, the company asked me to take care of the North-Western region as the Regional Head with Bombay as the headquarters. Thus, I was transferred to Bombay.

My Time in IOL Bombay

While at Bombay, I saw that the company was not taking the growth path while the industry itself was growing in the region.

IOL could not make any new investment because it was considered a monopoly by the Government. I studied the industrial gas industry and discovered that the country was running all its factory units very inefficiently and uneconomically and using a lot of energy per unit of production. IOL was the leader and all the others were following Indian Oxygen. IOL was using old high-pressure technology with high power consumption so were the others. If we adopted newer and better technologies like medium-pressure or low-pressure technology, we could reduce the power consumption by half. I made a presentation to the board and argued to change over to low-pressure technology. The board agreed with the proposal.

The company asked me to prepare a paper and make a presentation to the then Prime Minister Mr. Rajiv Gandhi about the benefits of using high technology. I did so. Mr. Gandhi had a very capable and intelligent person as Industry Secretary. He was Mr. S.M. Ghosh. Both of them understood the reasoning and implications and agreed to change Schedule 1 of the MRTP Act (The Monopolies and Restrictive Trade Practices Act. 1969).

This allowed modernization even by monopoly companies provided the new technology would reduce power consumption and the location of the factory was 50 kilometres away from the city in a suburban area. Their goal was to industrialize the rural areas of the country.

Presentation to the then Prime Minister, Mr. Rajiv Gandhi

Sensing that there could be growth, the company introduced a new department at headquarters called "Corporate Strategy and Planning" and asked me to head the division and develop the strategy for the growth of the company. Hence, I was transferred from Bombay to Calcutta after two and a half years of stay at Bombay.

My daughters were studying in a reputed school in Bombay. It was mid-session when I was transferred back to Kolkata. I told the company that I should have two offices and two residences-one at Bombay and the other at Kolkata, and be allowed to retain my present office and home in Bombay while I would operate from Calcutta and Bombay on a 50:50-timesharing basis till my daughters completed the present school session at Bombay. My daughters could then enter the new session at Calcutta next year. The company agreed.

As Head of Corporate Strategy and Planning

I did not study corporate strategy as a subject either at North Staffordshire Polytechnic (later it became known as Staffordshire University) or at Cranfield Business School. There was no such subject then. We were taught a subject called Corporate Planning or Long-Term Planning at Cranfield by Prof. Constable who was from Harvard. Incidentally, almost all the key professors at Cranfield came from Harvard.

Now, I had to conceive my way for Corporate Strategy at IOL. It was a great experience. During one of my visits to the UK, I discussed the subject with the head of Marketing, Mr. John Marshall.

We were discussing about the optimal size of an oxygen plant for India. All the UK plants at that time were of 1000 tons per day capacity with a maximum specific power of 0.75 KWH (specific power is the power consumed in KWH/cubic meter of product produced). He suggested that because of the low demand base, IOL should go for 100 tons per day plants with a specific power of 1.0. The demand for products in India was far too low at that time to justify very large plants. At that time, specific power of IOL plants were ranging from 2.75 KWH per cubic meter for plants of 63 cubic meter per hour (2 tons per day) to 1.7 KWH per cubic meter for 400 m^3/hour plants (12.5 tons/day) capacities respectively. 1.0 KWH specific power for 100 tpd plants would mean a huge reduction in power consumption.

I thought it through and conceived of a strategy of putting four large low-pressure plants of 100 tons per day in four locations at Jamshedpur, Bombay, Madras and Delhi to cover the entire country with cost-effective products. This would reduce the power cost of production substantially and the reduced price would increase the demand. This step would also reduce distribution cost and the number of people required.

At that time, it was difficult to get industrial gases to remote areas and if available, it was too costly due to the high distribution cost of cylindered gases. Our step would make liquid products available all over the country which could be cylinderised locally. This step would help industrialization in all parts of the country. Liquid supply in tankers was very cost-effective. Equitable development of the whole country was the Mantra of the central government at that time. Our plan was in line with government thinking.

We recruited a young person with a Ph.D degree, Dr. Ranjan Das as assistant manager to help me. He had just received his Fellowship (equivalent to Ph.D) from IIM-Ahmedabad in Corporate Strategy. He was helpful but he was more interested in focusing on long-term planning of existing business divisions. He was not very keen on expansion or diversification. I left him with the job of long-term plans of the existing businesses and I took on the task of expansion and diversification myself.

We applied to the Government of India for a license and received permission for all the four tonnage plants as I planned. The company was apprehensive about the quantum of actual demand and agreed to put up only two large plants to start with. One was to be located at Jamshedpur where we had the largest sales base at that time and the other at Bombay where the country was growing fast. These were the only two places where there were large industrial markets at that time. Although the government permission and IOL board approvals were obtained, the actual implementation had to be delayed till a new management came into being.

The then top management was risk-averse and did not want to invest too much money at a time as it would burden the company with high depreciation and extra cost of interest payment. This would reduce the book profit and affect dividend payment.

By that time, the expatriate Chairman and MD, Mr. K.D. Moore who came from the UK at the same time as me, retired and went back to the UK. In keeping with the then government policy of localization of top management, the company elevated the director of the largest division, the Gases Division. Mr. S.D. Singh to the MD position. The then Chairman and MD of Tata Steel, Mr. Rusi Modi was made the non-executive chairman of IOL. When Mr. Singh had joined the company, the company turnover was only 30 million rupees and now it was 300 million rupees. The profit quantum had always been 20% of revenue over the years.

He was happy with the present position and the parent company BOC (International) was equally happy. Even the shareholders were happy as they were getting a regular dividend year after year. BOC-International used to transfer all the spare old small low-technology plants from the UK to the subsidiary companies like Indian Oxygen at throw-away prices. Obviously, for Indian Oxygen, the depreciation and interest were almost zero. Indian Oxygen had a 70% market share in the country then. If any new investment were made, it would need interest payment on the new capital and there would be an additional depreciation burden. So, the book profit would go down substantially. Given this predicament, Mr. Singh did not take any decision for new investment although we had the license in hand from the Govt. to invest in new high technology plants.

Expansion and Growth of the Existing Divisions

Some actions through our Corporate Strategy group helped the existing businesses to grow to some degree. For the gases division, I made a collaboration agreement with a company in Delhi known as Superior Air Products. Our Delhi plant was too small and the market had started growing, particularly for medical gases. We needed products and they needed working capital. We made a deal with them whereby we would market their entire production at a predetermined price. Unfortunately, we offered a very low price, and the tie up did not last long.

We made another deal with a lamp manufacturer at Delhi, Sylvania and Luxman. They had a captive oxygen plant from which they were using only nitrogen. The co-product oxygen was being wasted. They also needed some working capital. We made a deal with them to sell their co-product, oxygen. After sometime this tie-up also fell through.

Jamshedpur and Bombay used to produce some liquid gases. The liquid market started increasing. The Gases division needed vacuum insulated stainless steel tanks for liquid gas storage and transportation. The Plant Division used to manufacture these tanks for us but they had limited capacity. We made a collaboration agreement with one of the engineering giants, L&T. They had sophisticated engineering production capability but no design knowledge for these tanks. We started getting these tanks known as VITTs (Vacuum Insulated Transport Tanks for liquid transportation) made by them. We gave them the designs and they made the tanks for us.

The country was in need of a new kind of electrodes. These were called continuous consumables in the coiled form known as MIG (Metal Inert Gas) wires. We developed a joint venture with MIDC (Maharashtra Industrial Development Corporation), an arm of Maharashtra Government to produce MIG wires. The name of the new company was Maharashtra Weldaids and my deputy Dr. Ranjan Das was sent to run this small outfit as Managing Director.

Thus, the company was able to see some growth both in Gases as well as in Welding. In the meantime, there was a vacuum in the Welding division and I was transferred there as Head-Welding Consumables and the Corporate Strategy Group was wound up.

My Time with IOL as Head of Welding Consumables (after Corporate Strategy)

When I was the Head of Gases Division Marketing, one day after a visit to Asansol, I complained to my Director, Mr. S.D. Singh that it was very difficult to sell the welding products because of poor quality. As he was not in charge of the Welding division then, he could not do anything. Now, he had become the MD in charge of all the divisions. So, he was planning to give the job to me to take care of the quality issue.

The Head of Welding Consumables, Mr. Kartik Basu fell seriously ill. There was a need for a replacement. He took this opportunity and transferred me as the Head of the division. I was asked to sort out the quality problem myself. I had no direct knowledge of welding or welding consumables although I was a metallurgist. I was a foundryman. After joining the welding consumables division, I looked at all the processes and decided to hold a meeting with all the Heads of Departments of welding consumables including the head of R&D, Mr. Ranajay Banerjee, a degree holder from B.E. College.

All of them said that the problem was one of selling and not of quality. I was not convinced by their answer. So, I called another meeting. This time, I invited all the Sales Managers of the Gases Division who were complaining about the welding products quality.

Apart from welding division people, I also invited some of our customers who had been complaining, to join. Moreover, I involved the Quality Assurance Agency of the Government into the process so that we could obtain a full picture from all the stakeholders.

It was a whole day program involving all the different stakeholders. Customers brought with them samples of poor-quality welding products which we had sold them. At the end of a full day of deliberations, the Departmental Heads of the Welding Consumables had to agree that there was indeed a problem. But they could not identify as to where it originated. Hence, they did not know how to solve the problem.

I called a meeting of all the foremen drawn from all the departments of the welding division. They were the actual shop floor people who were involved in the production process. Together with the foremen and Head of the Departments, we had another round of internal discussion and started brainstorming amongst ourselves. I asked each foreman to name five reasons why the problem was occurring. Different persons gave different replies. I picked ten reasons, which were most common amongst those suggested. I asked them to give ratings from 1 to 10 to each of these criterions in order of reducing priority. The main problem was finally identified as the corrosion of steel being used as raw material to make the welding electrodes.

That was the main culprit. I was then trying to figure out where the corrosion could be coming from. I found that we were storing around 1,600 tons of steel in coiled form at the open yard on the north side and these were carried by forklifts into the factory for use. There was a sulphuric acid factory by that side of our factory where the steel coils were being stored. My office was also on the first floor on that side and I often used to get a strong pungent smell. I did suspect the source of this smell was acid. Now, I was sure that that was the cause.

I met the head of the neighbouring factory and complained that he must do something to stop this acidic gas emission. He denied that he had any sulphuric acid gas emissions from his factory. I then approached the Pollution Control Department of the Government. They sent a team to investigate. Unfortunately, whenever the pollution control board inspectors used to visit their factory, they found no emission. Perhaps, they were working together to suppress this information. I decided to use a simple system called first-in-first-out (FIFO). I divided the entire open yard into four sections. This was the place where we used to keep heaps of steel.

I said that all the steel brought in the first week of the month should be placed in heap no. 1. Those brought during the second week should be stored in heap number 2 and so on. The workers were asked to consume the material from the first heap before they would be allowed to touch the material from the second heap. They had to finish the previous heap before using the material from the next heap. Thus, they introduced the FIFO system.

The quality of the products improved tremendously. Still, the problem with some of the customers continued. On inquiry, the foremen of the finished godown told me that this was because we were still selling some of the old products from the finished product godown where they did not use the first-in-first-out (FIFO) approach and some old stuff remained.

I went to the Managing Director and said that I would like to throw out all the 5 million pieces of old welding products kept at the warehouse as good stock. He told me that it was not possible. If I did so, the stock in the balance sheet would go down, and consequently, the book profit of the company would decrease tremendously.

He said that he would have difficulty in explaining to the Board as to why we had kept bad stock as good stock for so long. Our balance sheet was strong at that time. He suggested that I should find a place where I could keep these materials, salvage the good ones and sell them as second-rated quality—not at a time but within a period of two years so that we could write off the rejected materials over time and he would be able to absorb the impact of this loss. I did so.

I found a warehouse at Beliaghata where we had our old Research & Development (R&D) section. Now, all the finished goods sent to the factory warehouse were new ones made from recently procured raw material not corroded by acidic gas. Further, since we were also using the first-in-first-out (FIFO) method at the delivery stage, each fresh delivery comprised of only recently produced goods. I arranged a process of date stamping on the delivery-boxes so that everybody knew the manufacturing date. Both the production group at the welding factory and the sales group in the Gases Division were happy and so were the customers.

Having enjoyed some success through a branding exercise in the Gases Division, I thought of using a similar technique for the Welding Division as well. I found that our company had the maximum share of the cheapest product, known as 'Ferrospeed'. We had an overall market share of 18% in welding consumables. Our main competitor Advani-Oerlikon had a market share of 35%. This was because they were selling more exotic products with higher value per unit of sales. We were almost known as a low-end Ferrospeed company. These products were used by road side garages and repairers and not by Original Equipment Manufacturers (OEM).

We again had a brainstorming session with our managers, including the Sales Managers of the Gases Division. We found that the quality of the products was varying with the thickness of the welding rods. The thicker the electrode the better was the quality level. The electrodes used for sophisticated purposes were thicker. I gave them three brand names, 'Ferrospeed', 'Meridian', and 'Ferroweld' for the three distinct qualities. Ferrospeed and Ferroweld's names were already present. I discovered that there was a product-gap between these two qualities for some medium-quality jobs. We did not have any such product in our range and we were losing in that market. Advani Oerlikon had that product. It had a huge market and we were losing out. At my suggestion, our R&D developed that product and we branded it with the name, "Meridian". As a result, our market size improved considerably.

I found that some of the smaller companies were taking away a part of the Ferrospeed business for lower-end use by offering a thinner product than Ferrospeed, which was good enough for wayside repairing shops but not good enough for OEM (Original Equipment Manufacturer) use. It was cheaper than Ferrospeed. We had to find a low-cost alternative. We identified a small-scale manufacturer, Mr. Bhattacharya at Durgapur, a small town near Kolkata and collaborated with him to produce low-cost thin-grade

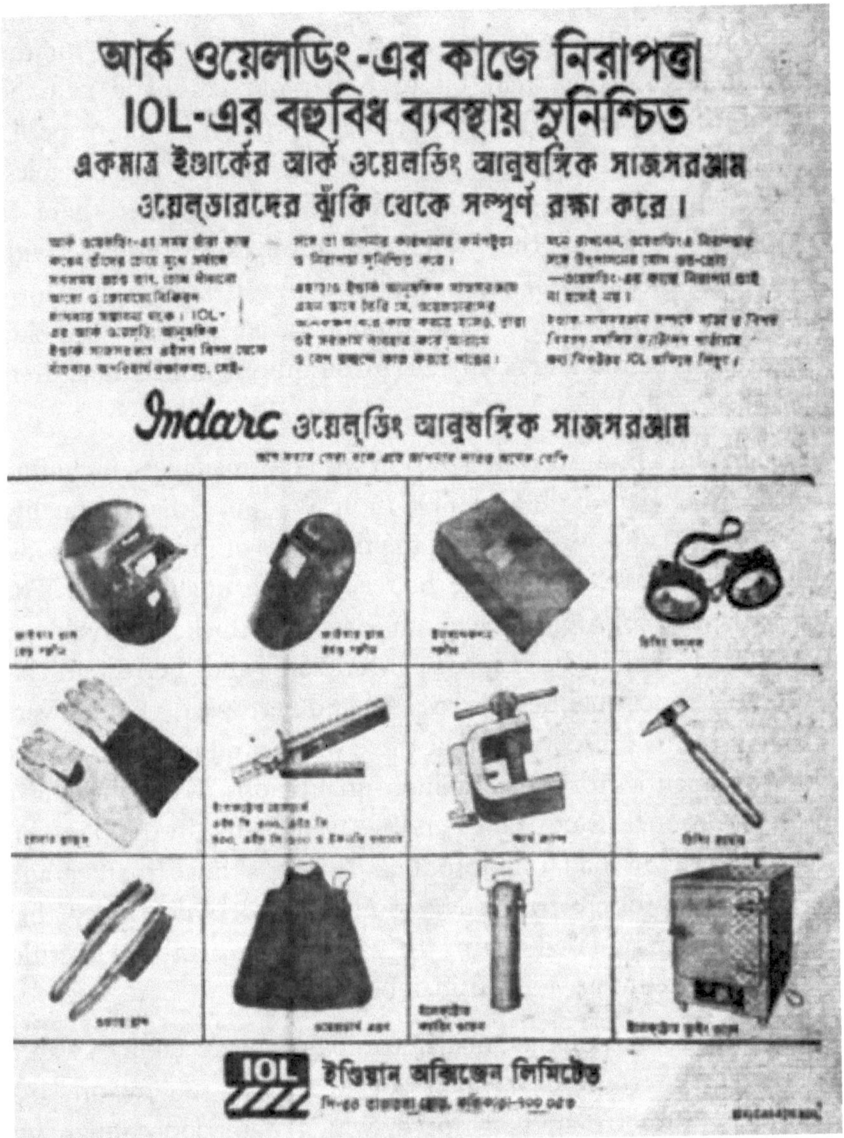

IOL Product Branding

electrodes. We transferred suitable manufacturing equipment and also provided the technology to produce these electrodes. We branded the new product, 'Indospeed'. In India, small-scale companies were exempted from 25% tax including excise duty and sales tax.

Hence, this product could now become affordable because we could reduce price due to lower cost of production. Now, we could enter this business at the lower end of the quality which hitherto, we had been losing to small-scale manufacturers. The overall sales and quality of the Welding Division improved dramatically.

Then I enquired if there were products being imported and not being made in the country. I discovered that the country was making battle tanks for the Defense Ministry that needed sophisticated welding materials. These were being imported from abroad. I asked the head of our R&D Department, Mr. Ranajay Banerjee, to analyse and find out what these electrodes were made of and whether we could produce these items in India. After a lot of research, our research team came up with a solution. These were essentially stainless steel based electrodes and we became successful in that market as well. This step saved a lot of foreign exchange for the country.

Then I came to know that there were many cases where welding had to be done with less heating. For example, if there was a breakdown of an equipment within the deep mines and one had to repair the item, it would be difficult to take a welding machine there with electric connections. Philips was manufacturing a special type of welding electrodes that could be done with low heat without using welding machines. We were producing the same products that was required but people would not buy from us. They preferred Phillips.

It was a lucrative business with very a high profit margin. Customers would not buy from us although our prices were one third of Phillips and the product was the same.

On analysis, I found out that Philips was not selling the product. They were in fact selling welding services. Whenever and where ever, there was an emergency need, customers could contact a local repair man of Phillips and get the job done. The bill for the service was far higher than the price of the welding electrode itself. It was acceptable to the customers because customers were able to get the items repaired anytime, anywhere, even if the breakdown happened in a remote area of the country.

In our case, the process was very long and bureaucratic. When a breakdown would happen in a remote place, the customer would send an inquiry to our sales office. If available off the shelf, the customer would then place an order. We would make the delivery to the remote area and the customer would have to find a specialized repairer for this job locally. Phillips had found out a better way to solve the problem. They identified a few welders in remote areas where the need existed, say near mines. These welders acted as small-scale entrepreneurs.

Phillips gave them welding materials in advance at no cost to them. They were to pay only when a repair job was done per service basis. Phillips also used to train these repairers for the job free of cost. So, the small-scale entrepreneurs who were welders themselves did not have to carry any inventory cost and were making a lot of money. The customers were also happy that a difficult repair job was being done very quickly in a remote area without any hassle. The money was not a matter of concern to them as they appreciated the quick service.

I followed Phillips's practice. I identified several good welders in remote areas, trained them well in stainless steel welding at low heat and offered the product. We used a new brand name for this service-product to differentiate from our stainless steel electrodes although the product was the same. We had now entered this new business area too.

I also came to know that we had another product called 'Ferroloid'. It was a low hydrogen electrode and was used for high-quality welding jobs. It was difficult to produce in our factory. The productivity rate of this material was 25% compared to that of 'Ferrospeed'. Hence the workers and even the shift managers used to love 'Ferrospeed' production as workers' incentives were based on production volume and not on the value of the product.

During my trips to Europe, I visited one of BOC's competitors in the welding business, ESAB in Sweden. They were a competitor to British Oxygen for the welding business worldwide. They were able to produce low-hydrogen electrodes in great volume easily. Being a competitor to ESAB, I was not supposed to meet them. But on one of my trips to Europe, I introduced myself to ESAB as the Head of the Welding Consumables of Indian Oxygen, as an independent company from India and expressed a desire for collaboration. ESAB showed interest as they had no presence in India. We had a supplier of high-quality iron powder in Sweden. This was used as a raw material for the manufacture of welding consumables. I told my MD that I wanted to meet them in connection with a problem regarding the quality of their supplies. He agreed. When I reached Copenhagen airport, ESAB sent a car to take me from the airport to Sweden. There was only a canal between Copenhagen and Sweden. Our car drove straight onto the ferry. The driver invited me to the deck and offered me a glass of Tuborg beer. By the time I finished drinking, we were already in Sweden. The next day, I visited their factory and found that many Indians were working there.

These Indian workers were successfully making low-hydrogen electrodes in big volumes at the ESAB factory without any problem.

On coming back, I confided to our Managing Director about my trip to ESAB. I said that we must change our production process of Ferroloid electrodes as our productivity was very low. I told him that I had obtained a few tips from the Indian workmen there. He did not discourage me. I asked my R&D Department to help develop this new process. We were only able to increase our productivity by 10 to 20%, but not more than that. So, I suggested to our Managing Director whether we could arrange a collaboration with ESAB. He agreed, but we faced an obstacle. British Oxygen UK was a global competitor to ESAB on welding consumables. He was not sure whether BOC-International would approve this step. ESAB was not a competitor of BOC in sophisticated welding equipment like Robotics. We approached BOC-International for permission to tie up for these specific equipment. They agreed. ESAB was the world leader in Welding Equipment Business. We thought that it would be a good idea to start some kind of association with ESAB and gradually we might get insight into their low hydrogen production process.

IOL decided to send a team to ESAB to discuss a collaboration about robotics. I and the director of the welding division, Mr. K.P. Deb met the top management at their headquarters in Stockholm and then visited their Robotic factory at Luxa near Gothenburg. More than 1,200 people were working there in Robotics production. They suggested that we collaborate with them and sell welding equipment based on Robotics to Russia. ESAB would send the parts in knocked-down condition to India. As an EEC member, ESAB was not allowed to sell its products to Russia directly. Our Managing Director liked this idea because BOC was not producing robotics and he thought that BOC would like the idea. Unfortunately, however, by that time, BOC-International sold their entire Welding Business including the one in India to ESAB. That was the end of my days at Welding Consumables which I had thoroughly enjoyed.

16

Back to the Gases Division

In the meantime, the Gases Division was experiencing a serious competition problem. This time, it was in Bombay region. It was the second-largest market for IOL in the Gas Business. They were already facing stiff competition from smaller companies but these were no match to IOL. But now they faced serious competition from a newcomer, called INOX (Industrial Oxygen). INOX had bought a second-hand low-pressure ASU (Air Separation Unit) plant from Japan. It was a tonnage plant with reduced cost of power consumption and the capital cost was also low as it was a second-hand plant. For air separation gases, power comprised of 65% of the total cost. So, INOX was in a position to offer a low price. The competitive situation was serious.

I was brought back to the Gases Division to head the marketing function again but this time the company elevated me to the rank of Deputy Chief Executive and asked me to take care of this new competition problem.

On assuming the new role, the first thing I did was to visit Bombay. While on the way to Bombay, I was reading the daily paper on the plane. There was an interesting news article. Tata Steel had just bought over a company called Special Steel Limited at Bombay. They were making exotic steel. It was situated at a place called Tarapur, midway between Bombay and Ahmedabad. On landing at the Bombay airport, I found that the Branch Manager, Mr. N. Moorthy had come to receive me at the airport. Once inside the car, I asked Mr. Moorthy whether he had ever visited Tarapur.

He said no. I said that I would like to go to Tarapur right away instead of checking in at the hotel. So, we started for Tarapur.

Upon reaching the Special Steel factory, I found that the physical transfer process between the two companies was taking place. The new MD of SSL selected from Tata Steel was seated face to face with the plant manager representing the old management of SSL.

While the handover process was going on, I asked them whether they had ever thought of using oxygen in steelmaking to increase the productivity. They said no. I asked them whether they would like to use oxygen. They answered yes. I asked them when they would like to start. They said yesterday. Immediately, I contacted our head office at Calcutta and asked them to transfer an 18000 litre VIE (Vacuum insulated Equipment—a customer storage tank) to SSL Works and we started selling liquid oxygen to them within 15 days. This was the beginning of acquiring new customers at Bombay through the sale of bulk liquid oxygen. Thereafter, we started focusing on large users and started supplying liquid oxygen to all of them. There was no going back on increasing sales and adding new customers since then. Soon, we regained the market share to our original position. Instead of depending on the sales of compressed oxygen, we started selling more and more liquid oxygen which increased our volume sales immensely and brought IOL out of danger.

Once the western region was out of the woods from the competitive situation and pressure in Mumbai, the company made me the Chief Executive of the Eastern Region.

This was the largest region then where we had just put up a 100 TPD (tons per day) liquid plant. The region needed an increase in sales volume to improve capacity utilisation.

On assuming the new role, I started looking for growth possibilities. One area was Health Care Gases and the other was Installation Engineering. In the former area, we gave attention to the ease of distribution and improvement in gas handling at the hospitals. I reckoned that this would automatically increase oxygen consumption per patient. We made bundles of cylinders packed together for bulk supply instead of supplying individual cylinders. We also introduced a new product, LMO (Liquid Medical Oxygen). This reduced the cost of handling oxygen cylinders at the hospitals. Most of the hospitals were using heavy weight individual cylinders. We introduced a system of pipelines to take gas to different parts of the hospital from the central liquid storage. That increased gas usage and hence our sales. Simultaneously, the Installation Engineering department concentrated on making new medical pipelines for hospitals giving access to oxygen to every department and every bed which had been difficult hitherto due to the difficulty in the physical transportation of heavy cylinders.

The medical industry segment had been increasing at the rate of 15% p.a. As a result, the business of not only medical gases increased but also the business of Installation Engineering soared. I was enjoying my stay in the Eastern Region with increasing sales and profitability till the parent company BOC started the process of Re-engineering. This meant the reduction of man power by streamlining operations and having people execute multiple operations and realigning the technical systems. As a concept, it was not wrong. But I felt bad as I had recruited many people myself telling them that there was a very good growth prospect in the company. Now, we had to let them go for no fault of their own.

Introduction of New Technology in the Gases Division and My Role as Chief Executive-Eastern Region

When Mr. S.D. Singh retired as MD, a new person joined Indian Oxygen from outside the company as MD. His name was Mr. S.B. Budhiraja. He had no past baggage, and he could take bold decisions and made new investments. Obviously, due to heavy depreciation and interest, the book profit came down drastically to only ₹ 2.5 million from ₹ 100 million/year which used to be our normal profit year upon year. In the meantime, BOC (UK) took over a company called Airco in the USA whose size was almost the same as BOC worldwide. In the deal, Mr. Dick Jiordano, the CEO of Airco was made the CEO of the combined BOC group including the operations in the US. The management focus of the entire company changed.

The previous management of BOC-International and hence of IOL was risk averse and did not seek growth or investment in high technology and was happy with the use of old technology and uneconomic old plants due to low depreciation and interest payment. Further, the previous management was apprehensive of the use of high technology as it would reduce the quantum of the labour force. The company was a happy and placid one with regular dividend-payment and having good labour relations. They did not want to disturb either the shareholders or the labour union and rock the boat. After Mr. Budhiraja joined, IOL decided to put up the first 100 TPD Oxygen plant at Jamshedpur replacing all the old plants with a combined capacity of 50 tons/day only. With this, the capacity in the Eastern region doubled overnight. The company needed someone to drive the demand. The company decided to elevate the status of the head of the region from Regional Manager to Chief Executive.

Thus, I was transferred from the position of Deputy Chief Executive-Marketing to Chief Executive-Eastern Region to run the Eastern Region as a profit centre.

Premature Retirement from IOL

Eastern region was the biggest region then. The region was almost 50% bigger than the North-Western region. It was at that time, an expatriate from the UK, Mr. Whittaker joined as the director of the Gases Division. Although, the government restricted the appointment of expatriates, it allowed some experts from the parent company to come to the associated companies. It was at that time that the new management of the BOC group adopted the policy of Re-engineering in all its subsidiaries including IOL. Due to this new policy of re-engineering, I was asked by my boss, Mr Whitataker to reduce the manpower of my region by 46 persons. Re-engineering meant a reduction in manpower by restructuring and reorganizing the work processes with the help of technology. I was very popular with all my workmen and I was even close to the union leaders. I selected 46 people whose sons' needed jobs, or whose daughters were to get married. The company offered them a golden hand shake as part of a Voluntary Retirement Scheme. All of them gladly agreed. Six months later, my boss came to me again and said that this was the era of re-engineering and BOC Group wanted to reduce more people. As a result, my quota of labour reduction in the Eastern region had been revised. The figure had become opposite of the previous figure of 46. That meant that the new target of labour reduction would be 64. I was unhappy because I was always pursuing growth and selected many capable new people myself. Anyway, I managed to persuade some more people to retire early and reached a figure of 63, one short of the target.

I looked at my appointment letter and found that there was a provision for premature retirement. By then, I qualified myself for premature retirement. I submitted a letter requesting my early retirement. I was only 53 years old then, 7 years short of full retirement. My boss was very unhappy. He sent our HR Head, Mr. Singh to talk to my wife to dissuade me from leaving. I did not agree. In the meantime, I received an offer from a medium sized Industrial Gas company in Kolkata belonging to Aditya Birla Group as the Senior Vice President.

The company wanted to expand and needed a person of my background. They offered me the same package which I was enjoying at IOL. I left Indian Oxygen but with a heavy heart.

17

Life after IOL

The Head of HR at Indian Oxygen tried very hard to persuade I and my wife to stay back at the company. I found that in the new liberalized Indian environment after 1991, there was scope for growth everywhere. British companies including IOL did not want to expand or innovate. Having lost the umbrage of the British empire, the UK companies were, perhaps, apprehensive of the Indian Govt.'s attitude towards them.

The Birlas were a very big Indian group. Out of all the Birla group companies, Aditya Birla group was the most progressive. So, I was happy to join an Aditya Birla Group company. The name of the company was Hindustan Gas Industries (HGI). It was involved in the production and sales of industrial gases.

In those days, the Government of India had been talking about 'Look East'. Mr. Aditya Birla was educated at MIT and was forward looking.

He saw opportunities in the East very early in the 1980s. By the time I joined the Aditya Birla group, they had manufacturing factories all over East Asia, including one at Johor Bahru near Singapore.

At Johor Bahru, they established the largest palm oil derivative factory in the world. The industrial gases company that I joined was relatively small and did not have a good technology base. I therefore thought it would be a good opportunity to find a progressive technological collaborator for HGI. I looked all over the world including Germany, Japan, US, France etc.

Finally, one company in the US called Praxair agreed to come to India and have a joint venture with the Birla's. We had a number of meetings both in India and in the USA. Finally, they agreed that we would have a joint venture called Birla Praxair, in which the Birlas would have 51% equity.

Unfortunately, Mr. Aditya Birla died in 1995 at the age of 50. I was not aware that he was suffering from prostate cancer. We had a meeting with him at Mumbai regarding the Praxair tie up to which he agreed. Unfortunately, he fell ill immediately after that meeting. He was taken to one of the best hospitals in USA for treatment.

He was treated there for a month. Finally, he passed away.

After his death, his only son Mr. Kumar Mangalam Birla became the chairman. He decided to sell all his small companies including HGI. He wanted to retain only the big companies. His philosophy was to operate only those companies where the company would be either number one or two or three in India. Therefore, he decided to sell HGI, where I worked, to Praxair.

The then Chairman of Praxair–Asia Pacific, Mr. Natarajan, insisted that I should sign the deal on behalf of the Birlas which I did with a broken heart.

Mr. Kumar Mangalam Birla graduated from the London Business School. During the five years that I spent at the group as Senior Vice President, Kumar attended all of our strategy meetings with his father but never spoke a word. He used to only listen. I was not sure about his leadership qualities and therefore I decided to leave the company.

All the senior management team told me that in Birlas, senior top management never retire and that I would be absorbed into any of the group companies.

I did not like the idea that I was responsible for selling a part of the company where I worked and yet I would still be in the group. I left Birlas.

Time after Aditya Birla Group

After the deal with Praxair, many companies in industrial gases felt that I was very good in dealing with foreign companies for collaboration. One such mid-sized company, Asiatic Oxygen Ltd. (AOL), approached me and offered me the position of Executive Vice President and asked me to try to arrange for a collaboration with Praxair. They offered me the same terms and conditions which I enjoyed at HGI. By then, I had developed very good relations with Praxair top management both in India and in the USA. They were willing to work with AOL as a joint venture. But Mr. B.K. Jalan, the Chairman of the company decided to sell off the company to Praxair.

When I was involved in selling HGI to Praxair, I had no idea how to value the company. There was neither any book on the topic, nor could consultants like S.R. Batliboy throw any light on the process of valuation.

They were using historical company data, which did not give a good value. The plants were old and the technology backdated. I thought that the buying company should look for future benefits rather than current assets. I showed them a bigger, optimistic picture of opportunities for Praxair in India. They were new to the country and accepted my views. Consequently, we were successful in obtaining a good value for HGI although we had old assets, old technology, and not a very good band of people.

In Asiatic, I took the same view and proposed a long-term10-year plan to Praxair. I showed how beneficial it would be for them to take over Asiatic's market share over and above what they had obtained from HGI. This would give them a very good base to compete with IOL. They bought my idea and paid very well to Asiatic as well.

After I sold AOL, I was without any job again and I was wondering what to do now. I decided to be an independent consultant. I named my company, "R.C. Bhattacharya Management Consultant" as a proprietary entity.

At that time, a small industrial gas company in the south invited me to be their consultant. They had an earlier consultant who was previously the head of IOL's plant division. But he had grown old and could no longer continue. I asked the company how much they were paying to the previous consultant. They named a figure. I replied that it was a pittance. They did not say anything. Later on, they sent me an appointment letter with four times the amount they were paying to the previous consultant. In this way, my consultancy started taking shape.

In the meantime, a company in the USA, Cryogenic Industries requested me to help them establish sales of their gas equipment and also advise them how to enter India to start a production base. They offered me a very good package in dollars and all the expenses related to my activity would be paid for separately. They suggested that they would pay to my younger daughter's account in USA in dollars so that I would not be required to pay any tax in India. I disagreed. I said that I would accept the money in India in dollars and would pay the necessary taxes. Now I had become a consultant to a foreign company as well. I was enjoying my consultancy days.

Part - VII

My Entry into Academics

INDIAN INSTITUTE OF MANAGEMENT CALCUTTA

18

My Entry into Academics

While I was with Indian Oxygen, one of the most recognized business schools in India, the Indian Institute of Management Calcutta (IIMC) invited me to be a Professor of Marketing. The demand for Industrial Marketing was growing. IIMC had no professor to teach Industrial Marketing. They came to know that I was a good industrial marketer. The then Director of IIMC, late Dr. Ramu Ayer offered me a full-time job as the head of the marketing department with the highest salary in the grade. Of course, it was lower than what I was getting at IOL. At that time, we were staying at a large IOL-owned apartment in an upscale location. IIMC offered me a smaller-sized apartment at their campus in the suburb of Calcutta at a place called, Joka. But I was seriously interested to enter academics. On weighing the offer and the implications and planning for my future retirement, I suggested to IIMC that I would like to teach during the weekends only, as a Visiting Professor, to which they reluctantly agreed. Thus, I entered the academic arena and started teaching Industrial Marketing on Saturdays and Sundays at IIMC. In this way, I retained my corporate job and started teaching as well.

Days of Teaching at IIM Calcutta

I started teaching industrial marketing from 1986 when there were no books on the subject. We did not have any subject like Industrial Marketing at Cranfield. Our Marketing professor had only once discussed one article on the topic. I wrote some points based on my own working knowledge and understanding. Then I studied as much of the scattered literature on the topic as possible from the IIMC library and made a subject content book for myself to teach the students at IIMC. I used to depend a lot on case studies particularly from my own experience and from recently published literature to explain the subject. It was an elective course. Luckily, my classes were always fully attended, popular and effective.

My younger daughter, Sumita was completing her graduation from Wharton Business School at that time. I used to visit her every year. Whenever I used to visit the USA, I used to study all the new books on management at Wharton Library. In 1991, I found a book on Services Marketing written by Berry and Parasuraman. It impressed me. I introduced Services Marketing at IIMC in 1991.

In 1992, I attended a short time course at Wharton on Strategic Management. Thereafter, I started teaching Strategic Marketing as well.

Initially, I was only teaching specialization subjects at IIMC. Sometime later, IIMC requested me to teach the core marketing subjects as well as the number of students had been increasing and they were still hiring new professors. By that time, I had opted for voluntary retirement from IOL and was working as an independent consultant. So, I had time to spare. Initially, I was given an appointment by IIMC for one year at a time. When Prof. Subir Chaudhuri joined as the Director of IIMC, he gave me an appointment for 5 years at a time as a part-time faculty. Over time, I became quite well-known as a Marketing Professor in the fraternity. I was getting calls to teach at other management schools like Jadavpur University, Burdwan University, Calcutta University, Army Institute of Management, etc. In fact, I had been teaching from the first batch of MBA classes at Jadavpur University (JU) from 1986. I was initiated there by one of my Cranfield friends, Dr. Tapan Ghosal who was a faculty at the Electric & Electronics Department of Jadavpur University. It was an evening program. Although I left my full-time job at IOL, I had been enjoying my new life as a freelance professor and consultant and had been doing well. A part-time consultancy job from a company called Cryogenic Industries, USA helped. They requested me to help them in their India entry strategy and market development as a consultant. I was happy to be a freelancer, working both in industry as well as in academics.

In 2002, I was invited by a little-known business school at that time, Globsyn Business School (GBS) to teach Strategic Management as a guest faculty. Perhaps, their chairman was aware of my role as the Head of Corporate Strategy & Planning at IOL implementing diversification and growth of IOL. I had a meeting with him at his invitation. He offered me a role to teach at GBS as a part-timer. So, I started teaching at GBS on an ad-hoc faculty basis from 2002.

Joining GBS as a Full-time Employee

Since I had been teaching from 1986 onwards, I had many students working in India and abroad.

One of my students, Dr. Rajdeep Buxi suggested that I meet the Chairman of Haldia Management Institute (HMI), Mr. Seth as they were looking for a Director for their business school at Haldia. This institute was 116 kilometers away from Kolkata. I met Mr. Seth at his Kolkata office at Ballygunge on his invitation. He agreed to make me the Director of the Institute. He said that I could stay in Kolkata and visit Haldia only twice a week by car. They agreed to provide for the transportation.

Once my discussion with the Chairman of HMI was over, I was waiting for the appointment letter, when I saw the Chairman of GBS (Globsyn Business School) emerging from Mr. Seth's room. On seeing me in the visitor's room, he asked what I was doing there. I told him that I was joining Haldia Management Institute as the Director and waiting for the appointment letter. He told me that I should join his school as the Director rather than joining HMI which was far from Kolkata. I told him that he should first ensure that I was the right person for his school. He answered that he had already considered this, and I was the right person for GBS.

I mentioned that I was going to visit my daughter in New York soon and would give my decision only on my return.

Meeting Chairman of GBS at HMI Office

The GBS chairman had a few philosophies that formed the tenets of the Globsyn Business School. One such philosophy was, "Ordinary persons could do Extra-ordinary things". Another philosophy was, "taking people to the next level," as their core values.

GBS considered itself as an autonomous body like the Ivy League colleges of USA. However, the school arranged for ISO 9000 certification of its academic processes through Bureau Veritas from the very beginning. This autonomous character helped them to think independently. I thought these ideas provided a strong foundation for the school.

At that time, about 200,000 students used to take the CAT (Common Admission Test) examination per year. This was a very difficult entry test like GMAT. IIMs used to select the best students from the list of those who achieved around 99 percentile in the CAT examination. This would have been around 2,000 to 3,000 students per year. I thought to myself, what should the others do who had scored less than 99 percentile but around 60–80 percentile? After liberalization in 1991, there was a huge growth in business activity. And the country needed thousands of managers at various levels. Everybody need not or could not be a Managing Director or CEO. Also, from my long experience, I had not come across any Managing Director who was First-class First or a Gold Medalist. They were, of course, all above-average individuals and good leaders and managers. Hence, I thought it would be a good idea to take in students in the 60 to 80 percentile range and groom them to compete with students from IIMs or other top business schools and succeed in life. It would give them an urge to aspire, fight and conquer.

On my return from New York, I agreed to join GBS Globsyn.

GBS was promoted by Globsyn Technologies Ltd. (GTL) which was started by Mr. Bikram Dasgupta. GTL was doing well in IT-related services providing value-added services to companies like IBM and others from Delhi.

He wanted to do something for his home state of West Bengal. He took over a failed company at Salt-Lake, Calcutta, and developed it into a quality training institution to impart 'finishing touches' to recently qualified engineers. He termed the campus, "Techno-Campus". The program was of six months duration called 'YSM' (Young Software Managers). This program was very successful.

Soon, many software companies started operations at Calcutta and needed engineers in bulk, trained in software programs. Unfortunately, Globsyn's intake capacity was limited. The software companies started recruiting in bulk directly from the engineering colleges and started their own training facilities and the demand for YSM waned.

Then Globsyn started Corporate Training for soft skills for large organisations. But the business demand and volume for this was restricted.

Being an entrepreneur, Mr. Dasgupta was looking for diversification in a related field. He realized there was a great need for good business schools in Calcutta. IIMC was one of the best Management Schools in the country. But it could accommodate only a limited number of students.

The business sector was expanding and there was opportunity for more business schools to enter.

Mr. Dasgupta decided to enter the education sector. GBS wanted to differentiate its business school from the competition. The focus was on Employability. GBS wanted its students to be corporate-savvy and called itself a Corporate Business School.

Thus, Globsyn Business School (GBS) was started in 2002. Instead of recruiting academic-focused faculty, it chose to hire qualified and experienced executives with an academic frame of mind and asked them to create a suitable curriculum. GBS developed a process of delivery that would groom "ordinary students to do extraordinary jobs". Faculty members were asked to impart knowledge from their own experience, apart from the textbooks, and use case studies as a method of academic delivery. GBS wanted its faculty to give the students a hands-on focus to be capable of performing at their jobs right from the first day at work.

Initial Vision, Mission and Objectives of GBS

Before I joined, I had been thinking about the possible vision, mission, and objectives of GBS. Sitting at my daughter's desk in New York, I wrote out what I thought could be the Vision, Mission and Objective of Globsyn Business School. On my return, I made a presentation to the chairman in the presence of the faculty team and shared with him my thinking. In the conference room of Techno-campus, I drew a big circle on the board. This circle represented his core philosophy. I said that we might like to add one or two ideas that were adaptable at the periphery while keeping the core philosophy intact.

I expressed the Vision, Mission and Objective of GBS as follows:

- ***Vision:*** To be a distinctive business school of choice.
- ***Mission:*** To prepare managerial leaders of tomorrow for success, in a competitive and changing world.
- ***Objective:*** To grow in size and diversity in related fields and continue to provide excellence in management education in the country.

These were enshrined as part of our school's credential presentation for many years.

Initial Composition of GBS Faculty

When I joined GBS as the Director, there were only five professors. The Dean was a post-graduate from IIM-Ahmedabad which was perhaps the number one business school in the country at that time. The Head of Finance was a post-graduate from IIM Calcutta. The Head of Marketing was a graduate from IIT, Kharagpur, and a post-graduate in management from IIM, Calcutta. The Head of HR was a lady with a post-graduate degree from XLRI which was the best-known HR school in the country. All these were very well-known institutions. Incidentally, the Head of Finance was recruited by me for his first job at Indian Oxygen. The Head of Marketing was a student of mine from IIM Calcutta. I found the working environment conducive. I was a post-graduate in Management from both Staffordshire University and the famous Cranfield Business School, UK. Together, we were a formidable team, and our chairman would often make mention of our faculty pedigree.

Academic Governance at GBS

Before I joined, GBS had a Governing Council and an Academic Council. These councils used to meet only infrequently. I introduced a four-tier academic governance system.

At the top, there was the Governing Council made up of top industrialists and top executives from Calcutta, and well-known academicians from India and abroad. The Governing Council's job was to decide the long-term strategy, top-level recruitments, finance and foreign collaborations. The Governing Council would meet twice a year.

The next tier would be the Academic Council. The members would consist of industrialists from Medium and Small-Enterprises, high-level working executives, and some faculties of eminence from local universities. The job of the Academic Council would be to maintain and improve the quality of the curriculum and method of academic delivery within the overall guidelines given by the Governing Council. They would meet once a quarter.

The third tier would be the Faculty Council. All the faculty members would be members of the council, chaired by the Director/Principal. Their job would be to implement all the recommendations made by the Academic Council and ensure that they were taking the school to the next level.

The final tier would be the Extended Faculty Council. This should be attended by not only the full-time faculty members, but also by visiting professors so that all were in alignment with the vision, mission, and objective of the school.

Reorganizing the Academic Governance Councils

When I joined, I found that Globsyn had a Governing Council (GC) that comprised mainly of IT professionals. Since most of them were from outside Kolkata and were heavily involved in their own jobs, the meetings were few and infrequent. I felt the team needed to represent the diversity of the industry and not be dominated by IT persons alone. I, therefore, started looking for top executives and other locals of importance. I managed to persuade the recently retired Deputy Chairman of the famous ITC group to become a member of GC. We invited the Chairman of Flakt-India, an ABB group company as another member. We were also able to bring on board the Vice Chairman of Texmaco, a well-known Birla company, as a member. Soon, we had people from FMCG, Electrical and Electronics (E&E), and Heavy Engineering in our Governing Council. These actions made us broad-based and gradually Globsyn garnered a good image and standing.

The Academic Council was mainly comprised of a few professors from IIMC. We brought an equal number of high-level executives from different disciplines like Marketing, HR, Finance, etc. The Executive Vice President of Finance of ITC group, President HR of Birla Corporation, Head of HR/IR of Tata Steel, an owner of export-oriented MSME (Medium-and-Small Enterprises) also joined as members of the Academic Council and the council discussions became more productive.

Method of Initial Accreditation

Globsyn started the first batch with 84 students. As time passed by, Globsyn programs became well-known, and our intake numbers increased to 120–150 per year. We were a standalone autonomous school with no external accreditation. Since our IT section was under ISO 9000 certification GBS wanted its business school processes to be certified by ISO 9000 as well. This was a good step.

Although GBS did not have any other external accreditation, ISO 9000 certification ensured some consistency in its academic processes.

Strengthening Corporate Relationships

Since the IOL days, I was active in CII (Confederation of Indian Industries). I was a member of many committees and was a known figure at CII. I observed that other educational institutions were not active at CII. GTL was a member of CII and BCC&I (Bengal Chamber of Commerce and Industry). I applied for membership in the West Bengal Committee of CII and was easily elected as I was well-known and GBS was the only educational institution that applied. After a couple of years, I offered myself for Membership of Eastern Regional Council of CII and remained active as a council member for quite a few years.

I also joined the Education and Skill Committee of BCC&I (Bengal Chamber of Commerce and Industry). I started attending meetings of MCCI (Merchant Chamber of Commerce and Industry) although Globsyn was not a member. The association represents mainly MSMEs. I thought it would be a good idea to remain in touch with MSMEs. At the invitation of CMA (Calcutta Management Association), I joined their Executive Council and became a life member of CMA on an individual basis. I also started attending meetings of AIMA (All India Management Association) through CMA. Our students started taking part in the programs of the Chambers. Over time through presence and interactions with these various associations, GBS gained recognition and was popular in the corporate sector.

Association of Indian Management Schools (AIMS)

Mr. Shantanu Ray, the then Director of ICFAI, Kolkata was the Vice President of Eastern Region (VP-ER) of AIMS. When he decided to move on from ICFAI, he requested me to take over the position from him. AIMS had four regions—East, West, North and South. I was elected unopposed and remained VP-ER of AIMS for five years. During that period, we organized a Deans and Directors Meeting of AIMS at GBS Salt Lake campus and it was very successful. Many eminent people like the director of XLRI, Dean-ISB, President of Welingker Institute etc. attended the occasion.

When I relinquished the position of Director at GBS, I withdrew from being on the AIMS board. About six years ago, AIMS started extending into other regions. One of the new regions was the Bengal Region. For the past 6 years, GBS has been the unopposed chairperson of the Bengal Region of AIMS. With this, GBS built a strong association with AIMS which is the only body representing management schools in the country.

Functions of a Management School

Management Schools should have four components—Teaching, Post-experience Executive Education (Management Development Program), Research and Creating Social Awareness in the community.

MDPs

The chairman had always wanted GBS to conduct Management Development Programs for practicing managers. But it had never happened before I joined. During my time at IIMC, I conducted more than 30 MDPs. This experience proved to be useful here. We began to conduct MDPs at GBS and held the programs at ITC Sonar, a prestigious hotel venue. We would get 25/30 participants for each program. These programs were successful both academically as well as financially. All of our faculty would pitch in. We would also invite a few external speakers. Apart from generating an alternative source of revenue, it increased the visibility of GBS in the corporate sector.

Research

GBS started as a Corporate Business School. The intention was to make the students employable. With that in mind, GBS hired experienced executives from the industry with an academic frame of mind. Later, as we became associated with various universities, we realized that research had to be an integral part of our activities. We began encouraging our existing faculty members to complete post-graduate doctoral studies or Ph.D. As a result, almost all the faculty members obtained Ph.Ds from one university or another. Unfortunately, many of them also left for better opportunities elsewhere, particularly outside Bengal. Today GBS recruits only Ph.Ds.

GBS publishes an annual world-class peer-reviewed journal GMJ (Globsyn Management Journal) and organizes an annual research conference called GMC (Globsyn Management Conference). Publishing high quality research papers has been made an important KRA for each faculty member. Students are also encouraged in research work. Thus, research has become an important activity at GBS now.

Growth of GBS

I saw the potential to extend the meaning of the name Globsyn to mean 'Global Synergy'. I began looking for foreign collaborations. I initiated the process by sending emails and letters to a number of foreign universities seeking collaboration but with limited success. Later, we expanded the search to more universities. Though there was no initial positive outcome, we continued the process and gradually started getting some replies.

In the meantime, the then Director of Globsyn Technologies, Mr. P.K. Ghosh, had been interacting with Jadavpur University (JU) and Calcutta University (CU) to conduct joint programs. Unfortunately, he died prematurely and could not bring any of

BUSINESS

Management Development Programme on

" PRINCIPLES OF FINANCE AND INTERFACES WITH OTHER FUNCTIONS"

NOVEMBER 16-17, 2006.

1st Row from Left : Mr. Suman Kanrar (Siemens), Mr. Rathindra C. Bose (Siemens), Ms. Shilpi Singh (Tata Motors) Ms. Anindita Basu (Hutch) Prof. Supriyo Chatterji (Head of Department - Information System , Globsyn Business School), Prof. D. P. Chattopadhyay (Head of Department - Human Resource, Globsyn Business School), Dr. Asit Naik (Medicenter), Prof. R. C. Bhattacharya (Director, Globsyn Business School), Mr. Partha Chatterjee (VP-Finance-ITC, Keynote Speaker), Prof. J. N. Mukhopadhyay (Dean,Faculty Development & Research, Globsyn Business School), Prof. Prabir Guha (Head of Department - Marketing, Globsyn Business School) Mr. Hirak Paul (Engineers International), Mr. P. Karmakar (F.Harley), Mr. Rupam Bhattacharya (Siemens), Mr. Suman Kalyan Ray (Siemens)

2nd Row from Left : Mr. Suraj Kumar (Globsyn Business School), Ms. Nilanjana Sinha (Globsyn Business School), Mr. Avik Ghosh (Siemens), Mr. Jyotirmoy Sarkar (Siemens), Mr. Prabal Bose (Siemens), Mr.Ajay Sundar (Lafarge), Mr. Gautam Bhattacharya (Electrosteel), Mr. Sujay Ganguly (Trigger Apparels Ltd.), Mr. Sanjoy Ganguly (Vesuvius India Ltd.), Mr. Ganapati Dalal (DPSC), Mr.Amit Bhattacharjee (Tata Motors), Mr. Himanshu Dhar (Tata Motors), Ms.Arpita Chowdhury (Globsyn Business School), Ms. Sayori Bal (Globsyn Business School), Mr. Partha Bhattacharya (Globsyn Business School), Mr. Sib Sankar Pal (Stolberg), Mr.Manab Saha (Stolberg), Mr. Sunil Kr. Rathi (PRIL), Mr. Kaushik Ghosh (PRIL), Mr. Dinesh Sharma (PRIL), Ms. Veena Vishwanathan (Globsyn Business School)

Organizing Management Development Programs for GBS

these programs to fruition. I took up the task after him and we finally succeeded in organizing joint programs. One such program with JU, was known as 'PGDSEBM' (Post-Graduate Diploma in Software Engineering and Business Management).

We used to select first-class grade engineers from JU. The technical topics, mainly software engineering was taught by professors from JU, and Globsyn took on management topics like Marketing, Finance and HR. This was very successful. We had another joint program with CU known as 'PGDAEIM' (Post-Graduate Diploma in Applied Economics and Information Management). Although we did not use the word 'Data Analytics' at that time, it was actually a program on Data Analytics. The statistics and mathematics components were taught by the Economics Department of CU while Globsyn faculty taught management topics including soft skills. It was also a very successful program. Our students began to receive very high salaried offers and jobs in analytics, in India and abroad.

Start of International Business Program

Next, we decided to expand into international programs. We came to know that the Indian Institute of Foreign Trade (IIFT) at Kolkata had limited seats but there were a large number of aspirants for the course. This was because India's foreign trade was fast expanding. The government had started several tax-free SEZs (Special Economic Zones) to motivate exporters. We started a new program called 'PGDIB' (Post-Graduate Diploma in International Business). For this program, we created a separate Academic Council with top bankers, exporters etc. The Head of IIFT, Kolkata was one of the members.

Revival of Executive Education

GBS chairman believed that there could be potential from young, upcoming successors of family businesses, aspiring for a Business

Management degree. We started a 2-year postgraduate program in management in the evenings for young business owners. GBS also started a program on Media Management for practicing persons from the media industry.

After I joined, I restarted Executive Management Education with an emphasis on young working executives. Knowing that there were a large number of working graduates in Calcutta, particularly with IT companies in Salt Lake who may aspire to get management education, we restarted the program and called it 'EPGDM' (Executive Post-Graduate Diploma in Management). Later, we changed the timing to weekends for the convenience of working executives. This was also very successful. We attracted 25/30 students per year. Some of our own employees also took advantage of this program.

At the request of one of the local stakeholders in Gujarat with good infrastructure, GBS ran a PGPM program successfully for three years at Ahmedabad but later this was abandoned due to differences with the collaborator on policy issues.

Foreign Collaborations

As I said, we had been constantly looking for foreign collaboration but with limited success. I believed that we could gain from their experience, scale up our operations and improve our brand image from these associations. We identified Coventry Business School, United Kingdom as one such potential collaborator. Coventry University was looking for collaboration and had handed the responsibility of searching for Indian partners to Professor Raj Shirole, a person of Indian origin. The Deputy British Consul in Calcutta gave me this information. I contacted Prof. Shirole and visited Coventry along with our present Trustee and Director, Mr. Rahul Dasgupta. We met the Coventry officials in the UK and signed a collaboration agreement. The agreement was that our postgraduate students could join their M.Sc. program after one year of study of PGDM at GBS in India. They would go to the UK and study there for six months and obtain their M.Sc. degree. The students would then come back and study for the remaining six months at GBS and would obtain our PGDM diploma as well. There was a provision that the students would be allowed to work in the United Kingdom for two years as an intern if they so wished. This was a good way for the students to recover the cost of study and obtain a UK degree.

During one of my personal trips to Scotland, I contacted the Director of Glasgow Business School. He was very keen to collaborate with us. We timed the visit to the UK in such a way that I and Mr. Rahul Dasgupta could go to Glasgow immediately after signing the agreement with Coventry. We did so and entered a collaboration agreement with Glasgow University for our PGDIB program. In this case, the students would go to Glasgow after one year of study with GBS and receive a M.Sc. degree from Glasgow Business School within six months. They would also receive an internship for two years in the UK. Thus, we arranged foreign collaboration for both of our main diplomas—PGDM and PGDIB.

Thanks to the effort of GBS chairman, Coventry University later agreed to start a joint program with GBS called MBM where apart from GBS faculty, Coventry faculty would come and teach at GBS, Kolkata. It was a one-year program, and the degree was awarded by the Coventry University.

Thanks to Coventry University, GBS being a partner institution, it was made a duly certified institution of QAA (Quality Assurance Agency) of the UK. This was quite an achievement.

As the brand image of Globsyn Business School improved and grew stronger, there was increasing demand for our courses from students. So, we started another program PGDIF (Post Graduate Diploma in Finance).

This time, our chairman focused on the USA. He arranged a collaboration agreement with Tulane University for our 'PGDIF' program. Tulane was well known for its Finance program. Some of the Tulane teachers would visit Kolkata and teach a few special topics. Towards the end of the two years program, the students would visit the USA for about 15 days and learn live NASDAQ operations in practice under Tulane University's guidance. This was also a successful program.

Our chairman was able to arrange a collaboration agreement with London University for their B.Sc. program under LSE (London School of Economics). Gaining acceptance from LSE was a great achievement. Unfortunately, this program did not gain acceptance among prospective students.

Accreditation from AICTE

Initially, GBS had thought to remain as a standalone, independent business school with its own accreditation. I also agreed that it was the best thing to develop ourselves as an Ivy League type college like Harvard, Wharton, etc. so that we could shape the system in our own way. Unfortunately, the middle-class people in India have more belief in courses that have government approval since employers in the government sector and even banking and insurance sectors prefer graduates from formally accredited schools.

The country has an approval granting body, known as the All India Council of Technical Education (AICTE). After witnessing the success of Globsyn, many other private sector schools started mushrooming in and around Calcutta. Some of them acquired approval from AICTE while others took the umbrage of existing universities. The fees of these schools were lower.

Moreover, due to industrial decadence in the East, there were fewer job opportunities in West Bengal. So, many students preferred to go to Pune, Delhi, Bangalore, etc. since there were many more job opportunities and students could more easily get jobs after completing their 'PGDM'. We were worried about our intake student numbers. So, it was considered best for us to go for AICTE approval.

Globsyn Business School AICTE Approved Campus (Amtala), Kolkata

Unfortunately, the AICTE authorities would not accept our present infrastructure at Salt Lake as they had a specific stipulation for the type and size of land and other requirements. Therefore, we had to look for another space in a suburban area. Finally, we acquired a suitable sized land at Amtala in the southern suburbs of Kolkata, 18 km. away from the main city. We constructed a magnificent infrastructure and started our present school in 2011 under AICTE accreditation. The commuting time was 1–2 hours each way from Kolkata. This became a handicap both for students as well as for the faculty.

During the first year of operation in the new location, we had only 32 students because we had received AICTE permission only two months before the start of the program. From the 5th year onwards, however, we reached our full capacity and there was no looking back thereafter.

For some time, we had been running two schools—the campus at Salt Lake Sector 5 with an autonomous diploma without external accreditation and the campus at Amtala with AICTE accreditation. The Salt Lake campus was running very successfully both because of the existing reputation and also because of the convenient location. The faculty being the same, we found it hard to run both the schools concurrently. We were concerned regarding the sustainability of the Amtala campus, as most of the students preferred Salt Lake to Amtala despite AICTE accreditation at the latter location.

GBS made huge investments in the Amtala campus and we had to make it a success. Ultimately, we closed down our Salt Lake campus and offered Amtala as the only venue. Slowly, the number of students at Amtala began to rise. We had sufficient capacity at Amtala but unfortunately, we lost a number of potential students to other schools at and near Salt Lake who preferred Salt Lake as the location. Many schools in Kolkata were not able to fill their campus capacity although many of them charged lower fees than Globsyn. Some have stopped their operations in due course. Perhaps, the success of GBS was due to the stature and credibility of Globsyn compared to other schools.

Managing Quality in Spite of Entrant Variability

Meanwhile, we had been thinking of how to ensure a consistent quality of our incoming students. Normally, we used to have a mix of students from high to moderate standards. We decided to introduce a Bachelor's program to develop our students from the bachelor's level itself before moving on to the post-graduate level. However, it could not be fructified.

Since the quality of our students varied, we made a policy of equalizing them by dividing the students into three segments. Our GPA marks ranged from zero to nine. Students would not get the diploma if her/his GPA was less than 5 out of 9. Initially, we were running the program on a trimester basis. At the end of each trimester, we used to divide our students into three groups: (1) Above six GPA, (2) GPA from five to six, and (3) GPA below five. We used to allocate these students to three mentors. Those who attained a six-plus GPA were to perform many other extra-curricular activities like debate, creative writing, conducting research, and excel so that they could compete with and win against students from the top-tier schools. Those who attained GPAs from five to six were divided into three groups. Those with GPAs near five were cautioned to be more focused else they could be moved into the third group with GPAs below five with the potential risk of low performance and hence fewer and less attractive options. Those with GPAs around six were told that they had the ability to move up and join the third group with GPAs above six and become managerial leaders of tomorrow with the opportunity to acquire better jobs. Those with GPAs of less than five were, in turn, divided into many groups depending on the subject in which they were weak and needed help. Some could be weak in economics, some in statistics, some in finance, etc.

Our faculty would give special tutorials to them so that they could at least pass the examination and get a reasonable entry job. Some of the students used to have psychological problems as well. They were entrusted to the student counselor. The student counselor had to deal with such students with compassion. That was how we had to manage our different students—developing them and nurturing them to be their best and compete with the best in their category.

Moving Upwards in Accreditation

After receiving the AICTE approval, we felt that we had to differentiate ourselves further as most schools now claimed AICTE accreditation. We, therefore, applied for accreditation from the National Board of Accreditation (NBA). One could not apply for this unless the school had been in existence for a minimum of five years under AICTE. Having crossed five years under AICTE, we applied for NBA. Although we had some hiccups at the beginning, we obtained the NBA accreditation, thanks to the efforts of the

Globsyn chairman. Only a fraction of the 3,500-odd private management schools in India has an NBA accreditation. This achievement further differentiated Globsyn Business School from other schools.

If one wanted to study Ph.D. in Management, one was required to have an MBA degree. An MBA degree could not be granted by an independent business school but could only be granted by a university. Hence, a Ph.D. aspirant from a stand-alone Business School needed a certificate of equivalence. Such equivalence certificates could be given by a body known as 'AIU' (Association of Indian Universities). Once a business school was approved by AICTE, and accredited by NBA, its students could be certified by AIU for MBA equivalence. This was an upward step for Globsyn.

Beyond Education—The Main Differentiator

Over time, we developed many aspects within our system, one of which was called BE (Beyond Education), by our chairman. Students were encouraged to be involved in Innovation through a program called Embryon. Besides this, every student had to do some social work for the elderly, disabled, and downtrodden under a foundation called Kalyani Foundation. The Chairman's wife, Mrs. Ranjana Dasgupta plays an active role in Kalyani Foundation activities. We also have a live project called Serendipity that is held every year. This is the brain child of the GBS chairman. At Serendipity, students perform in various creative areas like dance, song, music, debate, etc. in the presence of their parents and host a dinner for them. The money for this event is raised by the students themselves from corporate sponsored advertisements. Over time, Beyond Education (BE) has become a clear differentiator for GBS.

International Vision Seminars—Another Part of BE

We had been noticing increasing moral degradation in society not only in India but all over the world. Hence, we decided to start a series of international seminars on topics of serious concerns of the day. The Head of the Department of our HR discipline, Dr. D.P. Chattopadhyay had been a student of mine. He obtained his Ph.D. on the thesis topic of "Spirituality in Management". During my trips to my younger daughter, Sumita, I used to visit various business schools in or near New York. On such visits, I noticed much emphasis was recently being given to topics like Ethics and Values by universities like Harvard, Rutgers, etc. I felt this was a good topic to introduce in Globsyn Seminars. So in 2017, we organized an International Conference on "Spirituality in Management Education" at our campus at Amtala.

In 2018, we organized a similar program at Amtala on another contemporary topic, "Women Empowerment". On seeing this successful trend, our chairman gave these conferences a distinctive nomenclature, 'Vision Seminars'.

In 2019, we held the third International Vision Seminar on "Corporate Ethics and Responsible Leadership". Of late, Mr. Rahul Dasgupta, one of the two sons of our chairman has been spearheading the education wing of GBS as a Director and Trustee. He also gave impetus to these vision seminars.

The 4th vision seminar in 2020 was held on "Technology in Management in the age of Industry 4.0".

The 5th International Vision Seminar in 2021 had to be held digitally because of COVID-19. The subject this time was "Sustainability in the Age of Disruption". Esteemed academics like Prof. Dr. Dipak Jain, President-Europe, China-Europe International Business School, Prof. Sanjoy Gaur, Professor of Marketing, New York University, Prof. Mahendhiran S. Nair, Vice President-Research, Monash University, Malaysia, etc. were present. Importantly, representatives from the energy industry also made presentations, including the leading energy player of Malaysia—TNB or Tenaga Nasional Berhad. It was hugely successful.

The world has been facing the threat to existence due to Global Warming. According to Bill Gates, this is a bigger problem than Covid-19. Hence, the sixth vision seminar in 2022 was held on the topic, "ESG to SDG—A Roadmap for a Sustainable World". This was also held digitally.

Thus, international vision seminars have become an integral part of GBS activity in the Beyond Education sphere.

Looking East for Growth

In keeping with the government policy, we now started looking east for expansion.

Mr. Rahul Dasgupta has made a collaboration agreement with MUST (Malaysian University of Science and Technology), Kuala Lumpur. Now our PGPM-IB students are able to receive a global MBA from MUST which is a well-known university in Malaysia.

My Transition to the Position of Vice Chairman

During my stint as the director of GBS for 5 years, I tried to identify and provide opportunities to qualified Kolkatans working outside the state who wanted to return and settle in Kolkata. It gave them a chance to come back to their roots. Simultaneously, GBS would be able to obtain good people at less cost to the company (cost of living being lower in Kolkata) and the possibility of high retention.

One of my friends, Dr. J.J. Irani was the Managing Director of Tata Steel. He met me at one of the AGMs of All India Management Association (AIMA) in Delhi. He was the President of AIMA that year. He told me that there was a gentleman called Mr. Pratip Kar who was the Director of SEBI (Security Exchange Board of India). After retirement, he had been working with the Tata Management School at Pune for three years as Dean. Mr. Kar wished to settle down in Kolkata and was looking for an opportunity in academics.

I invited Mr. Kar to Calcutta Club and had dinner with him and his wife. He was an MBA from INSEAD and knowledgeable in Corporate Governance and had experience in Finance. At that time, I conceived of having three Centers of Excellence at GBS. One would be the Centre of Excellence for Strategy, the other would be the Centre of Excellence for Corporate Governance and Ethics and the third would be the Centre of Excellence for Finance. I thought Mr. Kar could be the ideal person to head the Centre of Excellence for Corporate Governance and Ethics. Having been at SEBI, he could ensure Governance and Ethics at GBS.

He could create a Centre of Excellence where we could motivate youngsters to conduct research on the topic and publish articles and papers on the subject. We could also start a Ph.D. program on the topic, for practicing managers. I arranged a meeting for him with our chairman.

When the chairman met Mr. Kar he felt that Mr. Kar could be a good Director for the school and suggested the position of Vice Chairman for me so that I could guide the Corporate and Business strategy and be relieved of the operational duties. Thus, I became the Vice Chairman of GBS since 2009.

Other Initiatives of Globsyn Director, Rahul Dasgupta

Looking at the future needs of modern management education, Mr. Rahul Dasgupta partnered with Harvard and introduced the HBS-Online course.

This was a significant initiative, specifically during the pandemic when virtual became the necessity for everyone, including students. He also introduced blockchain certification and this introduction was blessed by the ex-President of India, Sri Pranab Mukherjee. There are also plans to use AR and VR technology in content development. These steps will ensure Globsyn keeps pace with the changing needs of industry.

With Sri Pranab Mukherjee

Looking at the Future

I believe that my job now should be to mentor this institution to retain its present status and go for an even higher level through accreditation, such as AACSB (Association of Advance Collegiate Schools of Business) and other similar accreditation bodies in the world and thereby to grow the school to the next in size and diversity. GBS should try to grow under the leadership of the present Director and Trustee in related fields with a technology and research bias and be an excellent Institution of Higher Education with a human face over time.

My voyage at GBS continues but I do not know for how much longer.

PART - VIII

Eternal Search

19

The Eternal Search for Meaning in Life

They say Indians are, in general, spiritual and not materialistic. Indeed, the guiding principle and the philosophy followed by most Indians is that out of four PURUSHARTHs—Dharma, Artha, Kama and Moksha, the ultimate goal is to seek "Moksha" or liberation from the cycle of life—birth, death and re-birth as we know it and become one with the eternal.

In my life this search for the meaning of life and existence started very young. My maternal side of the family has always been rather spiritually inclined, more interested in prayer, reading holy scriptures and chanting Lord's name rather than worldly pleasures and attachment to family and wealth. My mother too was not worldly wise at all, preferring singing hymns, reading holy scriptures like the *Gita* and *Upanishads* than to household work and caring for the children. My earliest memory was of visiting a *bhajan* session (Prayer songs) in the late evening at our spacious hall that accommodated the outhouse deity and the villagers would attend the chanting and singing of religious hymns and I would listen intently from behind where the adults were seated, rocking back and forth in unison with the beat, happy and exhilarated, until my mother would find me, yank me by the ear and tell me to go to bed. Even after this, after our new settlement in Agartala, following our flight from Bangladesh post the traumatic post-partition riots and massacres in the 1950s, as I grew older, I would often visit the Shiva Mandir or Buddha temple to hear the lectures and learnings from various holy preachers and teachers, called Gurus, hoping to gain an idea of the meaning of existence. Why am I here? What is my purpose? Why must we all follow this path that each of us go through in a lifetime? What is the value of this existence? Where does all this lead to? One person who impressed me a lot was Dr. Mahanambrata Brahmachari. His explanation was lucid and simple.

I have always found, throughout my life, the ability to detach myself from any situation and look upon life and the various events that occur as an observer, and to question the purpose behind what was going on. Although I would involve myself in work and life with all seriousness and commitment, I could always look upon myself as an observer looking on.

Upon my arrival in Kolkata from Jamshedpur in 1963, I made new friends of my age. Three of us, all bachelors—a chemist, an engineer and myself, a metallurgist were just setting out in our professional life and curious about the future. Hence, we began to consult various astrologers to know more about our future. Our usual interest as most young men at that age have, was in when we could obtain— gari-Bari-sari, or in other words—a House, Car, Marriage proposal.

We were not really serious and often we used to look up famous astrologers and pretend that we were married with a family. We would go and ask them to predict how many more children we were expected to have. When the self-professed "famous" astrologer would answer solemnly "After this daughter, you will have two more sons", we would burst out in a roar of laughter having uncovered his false claims. Once, at one of these visits with an astrologer based in Kalighat in Kolkata, we made such a scene that we were chased out by the astrologer's stooges and barely saved ourselves by a whisker.

As the years went by, I got married, had my daughters, followed my dream of completing an MBA from overseas at Cranfield after working and studying in the UK for a few years and then returned to work back in India at the insistence of my wife who longed to go back home and see the family after 6 long years of being away. After all, she was the only child of her parents and thus it was a natural expectation. I had always been interested and often read books on philosophy, astrology or loved listening to the stories of various members who had become disciples of some of these Gurus that I mentioned earlier or had met well-known Gurus like Satya Sai Baba, Anandamayee Ma, Dhananjoy Das Kathia Baba, Babaji, Balak Brahmachari and others. I found myself drawn to meet these and more such persons across the country—seeking perhaps the truth, perhaps meaning of life, perhaps solace and peace. I visited many places all over the country, meeting various Gurus, even dragging my wife and daughters along with me, spending hours with other devotees for a glimpse, for a meeting—sometimes taking arduous journeys, with many hurdles of car breakdowns, feverish children, *et al.* I visited temples and many shrines, met many holy and learned men even, attending lectures with my daughters of persons like J.K. Krishmamurthy, and even meeting Brahmacharis from Ramakrishna Mission.

After years, I gave up the search, gave up going far and near. And after my first retirement, I began the search within myself. They say that every guru has his own disciple, just as every disciple must find his own Guru. So even though I finally ended up becoming a disciple of Balak Brahmachari after years of following Shirdi Sai Baba, when he whispered the Guru Mantra into my ear in response to my question of *"When will there be "Shanti" or peace in my life"*, I seem to have never really found my true Guru.

Hence, I turned to myself, to prayer, to the Greater Power and began to read anew the ancient spiritual books like Gita, Bhagawat and Brahmasutra and writings from sages like Adi Shankarachrya, Agyasta Muni etc., trying to find deeper meaning within its pages and words.

I pray for the good of the world and hope that I can become a better person, one day. I fail often. But I don't give up. I again, turn to my innate ability to resiliently be a bystander or rather spectator to the drama of my own life and pray that one day I could become better at my role and find peace within.

The search continues. I have, thankfully been successful and am deeply grateful for the material success in this life and have much gratitude for all that I have received but a part of me remains unfulfilled and incomplete as I carry on with my search for the meaning of life, the purpose of existence and the realization of ultimate peace and tranquility.

Eternal Song

Oh my lord! what nectar do you seek to drink by filling this body, mind and intellect of mine with life?

Through my eyes, I see and experience this wondrous universe created by you.

Silenced and amazed by the splendour of your creation, I long to hear your eternal song.

(*Source:* Unknown)

◇◇◇◇◇◇◇◇◇◇◇◇◇

END NOTE

All the views and opinions expressed in this book are solely those of the author. No one else is responsible for these views.